Testing the Market

Competitive Tendering for Government Services in Britain and Abroad

ROBERT CARNAGHAN
and
BARRY BRACEWELL-MILNES

Published by
INSTITUTE OF ECONOMIC AFFAIRS
1993

First published in February 1993 by

The Institute of Economic Affairs,
2 Lord North Street,
Westminster, London SW1P 3LB

© THE INSTITUTE OF ECONOMIC AFFAIRS 1993

Research Monograph 49

All rights reserved

ISSN 0073-9103
ISBN 0-255 36317-6

The Institute gratefully acknowledges financial support for its publications programme and other work from a generous benefaction by the late Alec and Beryl Warren.

Printed in Great Britain by
Goron Pro-Print Co. Ltd.,
Churchill Industrial Estate, Lancing, W. Sussex
Filmset in 'Berthold' Univers 9 on 11pt Medium

Contents

SEVEN:

LIST OF TABLES

Foreword

A feature of the trend towards privatisation in the 1980s and early 1990s was the government's attempt to enforce competitive tendering for some public services—compulsory competitive tendering (CCT). The intention was that for services which had, for one reason or another, to remain temporarily or permanently in the public sector, a market test should be applied. Where local authorities, central government departments and the National Health Service were using taxpayers' money to provide services which taxpayers were deemed to want, those services should be put out to tender. Depending on the results, the services might then be contracted out to the private sector: even if they were not, competition from the private sector would be likely to reduce the costs of continued government provision of the service. One might still question whether the services provided were in the quantities and of the qualities which taxpayers would freely have chosen: but at least market testing could be expected to improve the efficiency of provision.

In *Testing the Market: competitive tendering for government services in Britain and abroad*, Robert Carnaghan and Barry Bracewell-Milnes provide a compendious account of the growth of competitive tendering in Britain and make some fascinating comparisons with experience abroad. They review the extensive literature on the subject and show that, in general, expectations that competitive tendering would reduce the cost of service provision in Britain have been justified. Whether in local authorities, the Ministry of Defence or the National Health Service, substantial savings have been made either by the use of private contractors or by more efficient government direct provision under the pressure of competition from tendering. In the authors' words:

'... it is competition which encourages efficiency and which is a more important factor than the ownership of the successful contractor'. (p. 142)

In some other countries, government bodies have voluntarily chosen to invite tenders for service provision. But in Britain, central and local bureaucracies and associated unions have generally opposed competitive tendering. As the authors say of British local authorities:

'Many councils are more anxious to see themselves as model employers than as model suppliers of value-for-money services ... [and] some councils regard one of their major roles as being to provide a form of employment which they can protect ... from the capitalist world outside.' (p. 33)

Hence, unlike a number of other countries which the authors review, competitive tendering for local authority services in Britain has come about only because it has been enforced by central government.

Barriers to the entry of competitors have been raised—for instance, by increasing the size of contracts to put them out of reach of many potential competitors—so that '... in some areas of the country competitive tendering has been more nominal than real' (p. 76). Nevertheless, competitive tendering is spreading. For example, in local government, 8 per cent of spending is covered by CCT (compared with 1 per cent in 1988), and the Ministry of Defence increased the proportion of the work it places competitively from 36 per cent in 1982-83 to 67 per cent in 1989-90 and greatly reduced the proportion of 'cost-plus' contracts.

Any policy which involves contracting out may be affected by the Transfer of Undertakings (Protection of Employment) regulations since it is uncertain whether they apply to the rights of employees where work is contracted out. On the evidence, however, Carnaghan and Bracewell-Milnes believe there is scope for a considerable extension of competitive tendering. Even though it is not '... an automatic route to success' (p. 141), CCT '... has been vindicated by the inefficiency it has exposed and the results it has achieved'. (p. 142) There could, for instance, be an experiment in competitive tendering for management of schools and hospitals.

In drawing their conclusions (Chapter 7), the authors argue that it is time for government organisations to discover the consumer:

'If government and NHS consumers could take the money with them and buy elsewhere it would do wonders in changing the attitudes of authorities of all types.' (p. 145)

But so long as consumers remain captive, competitive tendering has a vital role to play in improving efficiency directly and in changing attitudes.

They conclude with 10 recommendations (summarised on the back cover) designed to take competitive tendering forward, ranging from changes of detail to proposals that apparent anticompetitive practices by government organisations should be investigated and to the suggestion that tendering should be extended, as it is in some other countries, to fire services and some aspects of police work.

The opinions expressed in this *Research Monograph* are those of the authors, not those of the Institute (which has no corporate view), its Trustees, Directors or Advisers. It is published as a scholarly piece of research which both provides a source of reference on competitive tendering and contributes to public understanding of methods of improving efficiency in an important sector of the economy.

February 1993   COLIN ROBINSON
Editorial Director, Institute of Economic Affairs;
University of Surrey

The Authors

ROBERT CARNAGHAN transferred from the science to the arts faculty at the University of Edinburgh, and completed a wide-ranging course of general education in the Scottish tradition to obtain the degree of Master of Arts. He spent 20 years in the Business Research Department of a leading electrical engineering company, and five years in commercial information in a medium-sized bank, with shorter periods involving other areas of work including research and writing. He is interested in many aspects of the functioning of the world, such as currencies, languages and the importance of variety to progress.

DR BARRY BRACEWELL-MILNES was educated at Uppingham, at New College, Oxford, where he read Classical Moderations and then changed to Economics, and at King's College, Cambridge, where he took his doctorate.

Dr Bracewell-Milnes now works as a consultant to academic and industrial bodies on government and international fiscal and economic policy. He was Economic Director of the Confederation of British Industry, 1968-73. Since leaving the CBI he has been Economic Adviser to The Institute of Directors.

He is the author of over a dozen books on taxation and other economic subjects, including *The Measurement of Fiscal Policy: An Analysis of Tax Systems in Terms of the Political Distinction between 'Right' and 'Left'* (1971), *Is Capital Taxation Fair? The Tradition and the Truth* (1974), and *The Taxation of Industry: Fiscal Barriers to the Creation of Wealth* (1981).

Dr Bracewell-Milnes's numerous writings for the IEA include: *Land and Heritage: The Public Interest in Personal Ownership* (Hobart Paper No. 93, 1982); *The Wealth of Giving* (Research Monograph No. 43, 1989); *Capital Gains Tax: Reform Through Abolition* (IEA Inquiry, No. 12, 1989); Introduction to *Which Road to Fiscal Neutrality?* (IEA Readings No. 32, 1990); 'Earmarking in Britain: Theory and Practice', in *The Case for Earmarked Taxes* (Research Monograph No. 46, 1991); and 'Capital Gains Tax: Reform Through Abolition', in *A Discredited Tax: The Capital Gains Tax Problem and Its Solution* (IEA Readings No. 38, 1992).

ONE

Monopoly and Competition in Government Services

In this chapter we consider some of the theoretical aspects of the subject of this study, briefly mention wider considerations, and refer to other areas for which competition has been proposed. In Chapter 2 we examine the purposes of competitive tendering in local government, as well as the support for and opposition to it. The principal legislation requiring compulsory competition in local government is examined in Chapter 3, as are the reactions of councils and of contractors. The results of competition for the provision of local government services are examined in detail in Chapter 4.

Next we turn to central government and the National Health Service, and describe in Chapter 5 the changes which have introduced new attitudes to competition in these vast organisations. Chapter 6 looks abroad and examines experience of competitive tendering and contracting out in other European countries, Japan and North America. In Chapter 7 we offer our conclusions and a list of recommendations. Finally, there is an extensive bibliography and a list of some organisations referred to in the text.

Although most of the material we have considered falls neatly into one chapter or another, some does not. For this reason, some of the sections in the earlier chapters, concerned principally with local government, deal with aspects of the subject which may also be of relevance in central government or the NHS.

Introduction

For whole economies, unqualified capitalism and unqualified socialism or collectivism are unattainable logical extremes. Even in Inca Peru and the Soviet Union, there were elements of private ownership and enterprise; even in the United Kingdom under Peel and Palmerston, there were elements of economic collectivism.

In pockets, nooks and crannies of economies, by contrast, it is possible for unadulterated capitalism to be tolerated and to prosper in nominally socialist polities: the Soviet black market in spare parts flourished *inter alia* because even high officials of the Communist Party recognised that otherwise they would never be able to have their goods repaired. Similarly, pure collectivism may flourish in pockets of nominally capitalist societies: in the absence of (compulsory) competitive tendering, municipal refuse collection and National Health Service activities come into this category, since the service is provided monopolistically in-house and the consumer pays nothing at the point of consumption.

The arguments against the monopolistic provision of services by the government are not new; but the tide of socialism has been ebbing in recent years, and the intellectual defences of government monopoly have been weakened and exposed. It is the purpose of this *Research Monograph* to compare the provision of services by state monopoly as against competitive businesses and to discuss the implications of this comparison for public policy.

Government as Purchaser

'I see it is impossible', wrote Samuel Pepys, 'for the King to have things done as cheap as other men'.[1] The fact that government still tends to pay over the odds presents an illuminating contrast with the theory of monopsony and the evidence of supermarkets, which owe their market share in part to the keen prices obtainable from their suppliers through the force of their centralised buying power. The explanation is that supermarkets are continually exposed to the test of their customers' making purchases on their own behalf and with their own money. By contrast, there is no consumer demand for services like hospital cleaning as such. When purchases are made by one person on behalf of another, there is normally a loss of efficiency. This is due partly to deficiencies of *knowledge* about the consumers' requirements and partly to deficiencies of *motivation* on the part of the decision-takers, who are not spending their own money and generally have no incentive to economise. When services are provided through taxation and not charged for at the point of consumption, there is no complete remedy for this inefficiency of purchasing; this is one of the arguments for charging.[2]

---

[1] *Diary*, 21 July 1662. The Thatcher Government launched an initiative in 1985-86 to remedy weaknesses in government purchasing. On 2 March 1992, Francis Maude (then Financial Secretary to the Treasury) announced in a written answer that savings under this programme had cumulated to £1,500 million.

[2] The benefits of charging at the point of consumption are the theme of Arthur Seldon's *Charge* (1977). We note below (p. 61) the possibility of specifying alternative standards of service in the tender document, which at least introduces an element of flexibility, although it is no substitute for decision-taking by the consumers themselves.

Government as Supplier

The government may not only deliver a service but provide it as well, although assumption of responsibility for the former need not imply the latter.[1] If the government is a provider, it is in effect purchasing from itself, as when one part of a firm provides a service for another. When a service is provided monopolistically by an arm of government and free at the point of consumption, the divorce from the market economy is complete. It is reasonable to expect the monopolist to exploit this situation, since the pressure of his self-interest is powerful and the countervailing pressures are weak or non-existent. 'The monopolists . . .', stated Adam Smith, 'raise their emoluments, whether they consist in *wages* or profit, greatly above their natural rate.'[2] Smith rightly applied the theory of monopoly to labour associations (such as trade unions and Direct Labour Organisations) as much as to commercial concerns. The benefits of monopoly may be extracted by either type of body in money terms (wages or profits) or non-money terms (comfortable working conditions, a quiet and carefree life). Whether the benefits of monopoly are extracted or destroyed by restrictive practices is a matter of definition.

Monopoly and Competition

The modern theory of monopoly[3] goes back to Alfred Marshall.[4] The total benefit of a monopoly is the sum of monopoly revenue and consumer's surplus. The profit-maximising condition that marginal revenue equals marginal cost, which is the same as under competition, implies for a monopolist a lower output and a higher price than for firms in a competitive market. If a nationalised or other monopoly seeks to maximise total benefit, output is larger and price lower than if it seeks to maximise profit.

There is thus a divergence of interest between the profit-maximising monopolist and the general public (including the monopolist). This may be seen most clearly from the example of the tax authority seeking to maximise the revenue from a particular tax, since the administrative cost of increasing the rate of tax is nil or

---

[1] The distinction between providing and enabling is the theme of Nicholas Ridley (1988).

[2] *The Wealth of Nations* (1776), Book I, Chapter VII, Everyman edition (London: J. M. Dent, 1975), p. 54 (emphasis added).

[3] We use the term 'monopoly' in its strict sense and not in the loose sense of a preponderant or substantial market share.

[4] *Principles of Economics* (1890), Book V, Chapter XIV.

negligible and marginal cost is therefore approximately zero. At the point of maximum revenue a small increase in the rate of tax yields nothing, so that marginal revenue is also zero. But consumer's surplus is being reduced at this point, so that the marginal social loss is the marginal loss of consumer's surplus. This social loss is reduced by a reduction in the rate of tax below the revenue-maximising level. The same conclusion holds good in commercial situations where marginal revenue and marginal cost are equal but positive at the point of maximum profit: the social loss is reduced by a reduction in the price below and an increase in output above the profit-maximising level.

This conclusion holds good for monopolies created by legislation as much as for natural monopolies and for labour monopolies as much as for commercial monopolies. It is borne out by numerous comparative studies of monopolies and competitive firms, of which a number within our subject area are cited in this paper.[1] Marshall's analysis uses the static concepts of neo-classical economics; but his conclusion is compatible with the dynamic analysis of the Austrian school, since monopoly discourages or prevents the pursuit of the public interest through the competitive search for better ways of doing things. More generally, the arguments against the creation and maintenance of domestic monopolies through legislation are closely analogous to the arguments for the superiority of international free trade over protection.

If a commercial monopoly is also a natural monopoly, analysis in terms of monopoly revenue and consumer's surplus may be all that is required. If the monopoly is the creature of legislation, however, like the municipal monopolies that are the main subject of the present paper, it damages another important element of the public interest, namely its potential competitors. At the theoretical level, a more comprehensive analysis is required that balances monopoly revenue not only against consumer's surplus but also against producer's surplus. At the practical level, the interests of producers and potential producers are the initial focus of this *Research Monograph*, since there is no direct consumer demand for the majority of the services in question. The loss of producer's surplus through legislative monopoly and free-at-the-point-of-consumption

---

[1] Monopoly revenue may be extracted in the form of overmanning and a protected working environment for managers and staff. Most British nationalised industries have been shown to have been heavily overmanned at the time of privatisation. The cost of this in low returns to the general public, the nominal owners of the nationalised industries, was spelt out in George Polanyi's pioneering study, *Comparative Returns from Investment in Nationalised Industries* (IEA, 1968).

provision is one of the most important and least recognised distortions in the British economy, amounting even on conservative assumptions to a loss of many thousands of millions of pounds each year in areas of the economy such as health, education and libraries.[1] The problem of state-subsidised provision free at the point of consumption is additional and complementary to that of cross-subsidisation of state 'enterprises' from moneys raised in taxation, which is a main concern of the present paper.

Finally, mention should be made of the argument for state monopoly that the tendering and other costs of competition are too high to be acceptable. Now, information costs can be high and a major consideration in the functioning of a market economy. But they are a price to be paid for a better result. Advertising costs are a case in point: we mention below books arguing that advertising is an agent of economic efficiency so long as it is not subsidised by the government. Whatever the best policy for competitive tendering may be, it cannot be that there should be *no* competitive tendering because of information costs. In a world where scarcity economics prevails, nothing comes free. In particular, the idea (common in collectivist circles after the War) that the government could borrow more cheaply for commercial purposes than private persons has been thoroughly discredited, not only by the borrowing experience of nationalised industries in Britain but also by the lending experience of British banks to sovereign debtors overseas.[2]

The Larger Picture: A Better and More Economical Service

The advantages of competitive tendering for public services are elements of a larger question: How can the services funded by taxation be provided more cheaply or at a higher level of quality or at some compromise between the two (a 'best buy')? More fundamentally, which services should be provided through taxation and which privately? And, where services are provided through

---

[1] One area of the economy where state-subsidised 'enterprise' posed little threat to producer's surplus was British Restaurants, a venture which collapsed of its own weight a few years after the Second World War. But it cannot be assumed that all ventures unsuitable for state subsidy and protection are so unsuitable that they will sink of their own weight and that those that do not do so are therefore acceptable.

[2] Information costs are an element of transaction costs, the economics of which has been analysed at the theoretical level by authors such as Oliver Williamson, notably in his 'Transaction-cost economics: the governance of contractual relations' (*The Journal of Law and Economics*, October 1979) and 'Internal Economic Organization', in *Perspectives on the Economics of Organization* (Lund University Institute of Economic Research, 1989).

17

taxation, should they be available on request or forced on unwilling recipients?[1] If the latter, they are not services of any kind in the ordinary sense of the term but rather resemble the unwanted 'services' provided for the taxpayer by the tax authorities or for parents by local authorities who remove their children in dawn raids on grounds that are rejected by the courts many months later.

The IEA and other bodies in Britain have addressed such questions over many years, and the following are among the ideas so generated.

It is doubtful if many services of social workers serve any useful purpose at all. In the late 1970s, 245 field social workers (excluding all supervisory staff) were employed by the London Borough of Tower Hamlets to satisfy the requirements of a population of 150,000 (one social worker per 612 inhabitants). When these 245 went on strike for 10 months, there is no evidence that any of their 'clients' suffered any loss or inconvenience as a result; some may have welcomed the respite from their unwanted attentions. Similar considerations hold good for any services provided on the initiative of the provider, especially if the 'client' is obliged to receive them whether he wants them or not.[2] Central government has been inept in monitoring local welfare services (Lait, 1980), not least because it has ignored the economics of bureaucracy and local government (Hartley and Marsland, 1980). Despite these failures of monitoring, direct government involvement would be even worse: maintenance of standards in services may be better ensured by government supervision than by government provision (Papps, 1975). Where services are to be provided by government, charging or voucher systems provide price signals and information comparable with those of a market economy (Maynard and King, 1972, p. 42; Seldon, 1977; ETPP, 1967).

The increase in competition is the principal benefit of privatisation (Veljanovski, 1989). There is little to be gained from replacing a nationalised monopoly by a private monopoly (Papps, 1975). The economics of bureaucracy and local government

---

[1] In an example well known to one of the authors, a wife who was also a General Practitioner deeply resented being obliged by law to open her front door to a Health Visitor shortly after the birth of her child. If Health Visitors are to serve the interest of customers or clients rather than their own or their employers', their services should not be compulsory.

[2] If social workers and health visitors are not simply serving the interests of their clients but checking that the latter are fulfilling their obligations to society, the boundary line between their work and that of the police is apparently being drawn in the wrong place.

shows that inefficiency is generated in the absence of competition (Hartley, 1980). The building industry is a particular case in point (Knox and Hennessy, 1966), which is one reason why council housing has been more expensive than it should have been (Gray, 1968). Attempts by bureaucrats and politicians to take business decisions outside the context of a business environment are more likely to produce losers than winners and losses than gains (Burton, 1983).

Competitive tendering is an element of government by contract (Mather, 1991). The generation of accurate prices can impose costs; but these costs are a necessary condition of the increased efficiency they make possible (Alchian, 1967); in a competitive market advertising costs pay for themselves similarly (Harris and Seldon, 1959, 1962).

'Every question of pricing is a question of property rights' (Alchian, 1967, p. 6). By comparison with direct collective provision, competitive tendering extends property rights: private persons have an interest in the business that wins the tender and in the assets of that business, whereas in government hands these capital values are destroyed by dilution (Bracewell-Milnes, 1982, Section III). Similarly, under collective provision, investment is either funded through taxation or constitutes an element of the public sector borrowing requirement, whereas under private provision investment is funded voluntarily. Wealth is created through the voluntary principle and destroyed through the use of coercion by government (Bracewell-Milnes, 1991, Part 2, Section 4).[1]

Competitive tendering is one of the many forms or dimensions of privatisation (Butler, 1988; Pirie, 1988). There has long been a case for replacing public provision with private alternatives in order to improve the quality of service (Forsyth, 1981; Shenfield et al., 1983).

The Scope for Competition

There is a broad range of local authority and other government services that lend themselves to privatisation and competition, through competitive tendering or otherwise. Among local authority services, the Adam Smith Institute in 1982 discussed the contracting out of chartered accountancy, security, data processing, house valuation and sales, architects and planning, refuse and

---

[1] The argument is not invalidated by the element of compulsion in compulsory competitive tendering, which may be required to offset imperfections in the political market, where the agents are spending other people's money and not their own.

cleansing, highways management, pest control, care of the elderly and leisure facilities (WWC, 1982). It has since issued publications *inter alia* on firefighting (Simmonds, 1989), prison management (Elliott, 1988; Young, 1987), the funding of roads (Butler, 1982), the management of NHS hospitals (Davis, D., 1985), and care of the elderly (Pirie and Butler, 1989).[1]

Among further developments in 1992, a White Paper proposed the extension of compulsory competitive tendering to white collar services in local government (CQ, 1991). In a speech on 3 March to the Adam Smith Institute conference on contracting out for central government services, Francis Maude, Financial Secretary to the Treasury, mentioned

> 'accounting, audit, inspection and review, legal, operational research and project management; executive and clerical operation to include payments of grants and subsidies, advisory services, data collection, counter operations and payroll' (Maude, 1992).

The Federation of Civil Engineering Contractors pressed the government to introduce compulsory competitive tendering for railway infrastructure contracts. The British Broadcasting Corporation invited private contractors to tender for work ranging from set design and wardrobes to film editing. Sir George Young, Housing and Planning Minister, announced that council tenants in England would have the right to take over the management of their estates, as an element of a new government programme to force councils to put the management of council estates out to compulsory competitive tendering.

In most of the contracting out that has been achieved or adumbrated by the Thatcher and Major administrations, the emphasis has been on the efficient and economical satisfaction of a local or central government specification. There has been little recognition of the fact that individuals' preferences may differ widely. This is more significant in some areas of policy than in others. People may have much the same ideas of what it is to be healthy (though not of the relative merits of different forms of treatment); but in education, for example, disagreement runs deep on almost everything. In these circumstances, the straitjacket of a National Curriculum is unlikely to bear much resemblance to what customers would choose in a market economy. There is no reason other than harmonisation, standardisation and centralisation why Latin and Greek should not be optional core subjects within the

---

[1] This is also the theme of C. S. B. Galasko, Ian McColl and Caroline Lipkin, *Competing for the Disabled*, London: IEA Health and Welfare Unit, 1989.

National Curriculum, which is in effect what they have been for centuries, instead of being banished to the periphery. The Department of Education seems never to have heard of the principle of 'subsidiarity'.

Ultimately, the only answer is to empower the customers with the use of their own money, through tax relief, vouchers or otherwise. But even within the constraints of the existing system, different schools and examination boards could offer widely differing products, funded from taxation but subject to much less centralised control than at present: for example, a school's funding might depend on a mixture of examination results and one or more proxies for value added or parental satisfaction. This is a variant of the idea of contracting out and gives an indication of how widely the idea can be applied; the current policy of enabling schools to opt out of local authority control extends the scope for more radical devolution.

Conclusion

Although the rest of this *Research Monograph* is primarily concerned with the technicalities of competitive tendering, we do not regard this as a technical subject standing by itself. It is part of a larger whole concerned with economy and efficiency in government spending (the 'best buy') and, more fundamentally, the satisfaction of the requirements of the individual, whether within the constraints of the present free-at-the-point-of-consumption system or under the liberation of a system empowering the customer to register his own preferences with his own money, through tax relief, vouchers or otherwise.

TWO

Competitive Tendering and Local Authorities

This chapter examines the purposes of competitive tendering in the context of the growth of local government services in Britain, and the 1980 Act which first made tendering compulsory for a few of these services. Also considered are direct labour organisations, and the growth of competitive tendering and of opposition to it. Finally, there is a short note on the European Community's requirements in this connection.

Local Authorities

Competitive tendering is the offering of tenders by several potential suppliers in competition with one another. Contracting out, in the present context, is the purchase (by contract) of requirements from an outside supplier—in contrast to using in-house resources to provide these requirements. Competitive tendering and contracting out, for the provision of government services, are related but distinct matters. Contracting out can be a result of competitive tendering, but both also take place independently of each other. While there is nothing new about either of these processes in the public sector, there are many areas of government in which neither has, until recent years, been applied to any significant extent, if at all.

Expansion of Activities

For many years it has been traditional in local authorities to provide services to the public by employing staff directly. With the expansion of their functions, local authorities have become both spenders and employers on a large scale. The proportion of the employed labour force working for local government expanded from 1·2 per cent in 1890 to 5·6 per cent in 1938 and to over 12 per cent in 1982 (Butler, 1985, p. 349). Local authorities now employ 2·3 million people (virtually 10 per cent of the total workforce), and spend some £48,000 million a year (PA, p. 1). Their total spending accounts for a quarter of all public-sector spending

(Ridley, 1988, p. 14, and Digings, 1991, p. 173). They spend some £3,000 million a year on buying in goods and services of many types (AC87, p. 1). Local government is not, however, in general highly regarded by the public. It is said, for example, that 'people tend to have a poor impression of councils, regarding them as remote, bureaucratic, old-fashioned and bungling' (PCR, p. 16).

The expansion of local government activities was due partly to encouragement or legislation by central government, and partly to the development of local authorities' own ambitions to expand their role in providing services to their communities.[1] Since one reason for the expansion of local government was a vogue for municipal socialism, it was natural that each authority employed directly the staff needed to provide these services. Municipal socialists were not restricted to one political party. Liverpool Conservatives, for example, in the early years of this century endorsed local government provision of tramways, electricity and even a zoo (Ridley, p. 30). By providing services free to the consumer, or on a subsidised basis, or by making life difficult for private competitors in other ways, councils came to monopolise provision of a variety of services. There is no inherent reason why the lending of books or the collection of rubbish should be a municipal monopoly any more than the delivery of milk or the renting of television sets. They have become so because, for good or bad reasons, central and local governments decided to provide certain services on a free-for-all basis. It has taken a very long time for the question to be asked as to whether this should also require the production of such services to be in the hands of local government employees.

Monopoly and Uniformity

One consequence of the monopoly provision of certain services by local authorities has often been the assumption that services must be universal and uniform. Michael Clarke and John Stewart point out that

'public provision has limited choice, because universality sees no need for choice and uniformity no case for the diversity from which choice is made. ... for most of local government there has been too little exploration either of the diversity of need or the possibility of diversity of provision. Uniformity has been its own justification. It is a difference that has had to be justified. This has, of course, reinforced the idea of local authorities being universal providers since only in this way is it believed possible to ensure uniformity' (Clarke and Stewart, 1989b, pp. 6-7).

---

[1] For example, local authorities in England and Wales operate up to 1,800 indoor sports and leisure centres, in addition to 250 golf courses and a host of outdoor sports facilities (McGuirk, 1992, p. 55).

23

Another consequence has been the belief that bigger authorities are better than small ones, a notion that derives largely from the assumption that councils must themselves produce the services they provide. As Clarke and Stewart have written:

'For many years it has been assumed that if local authorities are given responsibility for a service, they should provide that service directly through their own organisation and should themselves employ all the staff and own all the resources required for the provision of services. . . . The assumption has meant not merely that local authorities have rarely considered contracting out their services or the wide-scale use of voluntary provision, but that even joint action between authorities has rarely been seen as a practical option. . . . It has meant, too, that in the long and unproductive debates about local government re-organisation, the size of local authorities has been assumed to be governed by the necessities of direct provision, rather than by, say, perceptions of local community. It has even been argued that the size of local authorities should be governed by their capacity to employ specialist staff or deploy specialist services' (Clarke and Stewart, 1989b, p. 4).

However, in recent years there has been some change in attitudes towards the concentration of power and wealth in the hands of officials and politicians, at least as regards local government. As the Audit Commission has expressed it:

'An implicit belief in the ability of large-scale public bureaucracies to solve social problems has been replaced by scepticism, doubt and willingness to experiment with other methods. There are ever louder calls for more responsive structures and more local flexibility' (AC88a, p. 1).

There are 514 local authorities in Britain. Of these, 404 are in England: 39 county councils, 32 London borough councils, the City of London, 36 metropolitan district (or borough) councils, and 296 district councils. In Scotland there are nine regional councils, three island councils, and 53 district councils. Wales has eight county councils and 37 district councils.

The Purposes of Competitive Tendering

Improved Efficiency

The primary purpose of competitive tendering is to obtain better value for taxpayers' money by reducing expenses, improving services or both. The biggest impediment to efficiency is monopoly, which in the context of local government can bring problems such as complacency, insufficient regard to costs, and an overall disregard for value for money (PCR, p. 19). The main aim, that of improving the value obtained for spending on government services, does not require contracting out as a necessary outcome. As we shall see later, it is competition rather than ownership which is the more important factor in obtaining efficiency.

As David Hunt has pointed out, the 1980 Act reflected the need to ensure that the role of those who actually deliver services be made quite separate and distinct from the role of government, whether local or central. If this distinction is not made clear there is the danger that the thinking, and the interests, of those who are providing the service will be taken to stand for the interests and needs of the public for whom and to whom the service is being delivered (TT, 1990, p. 8).

Other Aims

Joe Painter explains the legislation as being motivated mainly by the government's general aims of cutting public expenditure, reducing the size of the public sector in the economy and constraining the power of the trade unions. He writes that

'The government argues that local authorities should not be able to use their relative autonomy from the central state to increase public expenditure or retain service production in the public sector when central government policy is to reduce both public expenditure and the size of the public sector.'

Furthermore, 'The high levels of unionisation in the public sector are considered to be a major reason for both the growth in its costs and poor standards of service' (Painter, 1990, pp. 3-4).

In 1988 Nicholas Ridley stated:

'Since 1979 the present Government has had two overriding objectives in relation to local government. First, it has been essential to constrain the growth of local authority expenditure in order to stop it taking an ever-larger proportion of the total national product at the expense of other areas of the economy. Secondly, it has remained as important as ever to maintain and enhance the quality of those local authority services which the public really needs' (Ridley, p. 7).

Clearly one possible aim of competitive tendering, that of reducing the number of government employees, can be met only by contracting out or some variant thereof.

The Enabling Council

Michael Clarke and John Stewart point out that

'The focus needs to be changed from one that is inward on the organisation of service to one which is outward to the community. In the enabling council the emphasis of the councillor must be less on the workings of the services provided and more on the needs and problems to be met and whether they are effectively being met' (Clarke and Stewart, 1989a, p. 13).

There are six basic reasons for governments considering use of the private sector to help deliver services (based on an analysis of the American situation by Harry P. Hatry—Allen, pp. 2-4):

1. To obtain special skills or supplement staff for short periods.
2. To meet demands beyond current government capacity.
3. To reduce costs.
4. To improve service quality.
5. To provide clients with more choice of providers and levels of service.
6. For ideological reasons, on the basis that the less governments do, the better.

Advantages and Disadvantages

As seen by the Audit Commission, the advantages and disadvantages of contracting out can be expressed as follows (AC87, p. 5):

Advantages:

Generally lower costs

Tighter financial control

Reduced management 'load'

Clear service standards

'Competitive' ethos

Disadvantages:

Less direct control

Less flexibility in use of DLO staff

Increased overheads
—letting the contract
—maintaining performance

Risk of exploitation once DLO is disbanded.

Although control naturally becomes less direct, this does not imply that it becomes less effective, and a similar distinction should be made in respect of flexibility. For example, in the private sector it is normal for companies to include in a contract clauses that penalise the supplier for not meeting requirements on time; this would be much harder to do with internal staff (Meredith, 1992, p. 226). There are, of course, costs involved, and whether tendering is a good option to choose will depend largely on whether such costs are met or exceeded by any savings obtained. The risks of exploitation once a council is dependent on outside contractors will depend on the degree of competition which remains after disbanding of DLOs. These, and other aspects of the results of competitive tendering in practice, will be examined in later sections.

Attitudes towards contracting out, or more generally to 'out-sourcing' (for either goods or services), may be changing in the private sector. Of the top 100 computer users, 66 per cent were opposed to 'out-sourcing' in 1989, whilst in 1991 as many as 65·5 per cent had no objection to the idea. However, it is said that the concept appeals, at least in the computer business, only to the people responsible for the overall success of a concern, and not to those managers for whom 'it's too much of a threat to them and their empire' (Meredith, p. 225).

The 1980 Act

The Local Government, Planning and Land Act 1980 (LGPLA) deals with many matters. Here we are concerned only with Part III which covers direct labour organisations (DLOs). The inefficiency and lack of accountability of DLOs has been a source of widespread concern, and the Labour Government of 1974-79 intended to deal with the problem. In 1976 the Minister of Housing issued a Green Paper proposing a reform of local authorities' DLOs and suggesting competitive tendering (IDS, p. 5). In November 1978 the Parliamentary Under-Secretary of State at the Department of the Environment stated that future legislation on DLOs would be designed to improve their accountability and create conditions in which they could become more truly comparable with private contractors. He added that 'legislation will provide controls to ensure that consistently inefficient DLOs are not tolerated'. In 1978 a working party of local authority, district audit and Department of the Environment representatives produced recommendations on the use of competition. The May 1979 election prevented the Labour Government from introducing legislation, but the new Conservative Government issued a consultation paper outlining their own proposals which were later embodied in Part III of the 1980 Act. This came into operation on 1 April 1981 in England and Wales, and on 1 April 1982 in Scotland (Winetrobe and Nield, p. 13, and PCLG, 1991, p. 1).

Work Covered by the Act

The 1980 Act required compulsory competition in a proportion of non-emergency construction and maintenance work on

27

highways and buildings, specifically for the following areas (PCLG, p. 1):

o general building maintenance work;

o major new construction work (exceeding £50,000);

o minor new construction work (not exceeding £50,000);

o general highways work (construction and maintenance work, snow clearance, maintenance of street lighting).

Local authorities were allowed to use their own direct labour for part of this work only in competition with outside suppliers. Thresholds were set for the value of contracts above which authorities had to put all work out to tender. Below the thresholds, a certain proportion of expenditure did not have to be open to competition. Both the threshold and the proportion of work which could be awarded in-house without competition depended on the category of work (general highways, general water and sewerage, other new construction, or maintenance work). These thresholds and proportions were changed by stages, gradually exposing more work to competition. Changes were made by regulations issued under the Act in 1981, 1982, 1983, 1987 and 1988 (IDS, p. 18, and AC91a, pp. 2-3). As from October 1989, the limits for general maintenance and new construction work were abolished, so that all such work became open to competition. In July 1991 the Government began consultation on a proposal that the limits for general highways work should also be abolished. DLOs with less than 30 employees were exempt from compulsory competition until October 1989, when the size below which exemption applied was reduced to 15 employees (PCLG, 1991, p. 2).

Accounts and Targets

Authorities were obliged to introduce separate accounts for DLO work on sewerage, highways, new building work and maintenance (CBI2, 1988, p. 18). Direct labour organisations which kept the right to do the work had to make a trading surplus in each financial year equivalent to a specified rate of return on capital, based on current-cost accounting, as directed by the Secretary of State. This rate of return was set in 1981 at 5 per cent. Failure to achieve this rate in three (from 1987, two) consecutive years obliged a local authority or development body to send a report on the matter to the Secretary of State. The Secretary of State had powers to call for a special report from an authority on their construction and maintenance work during the three preceding years, and such reports had been requested from 14 authorities by 1987. He also had powers, after requesting a special report, to direct them to cease such work. Four DLOs have closed down as a result of being unable to meet the Act's requirements (Winetrobe, p. 14, IDS, p. 18). However, this sanction has been replaced by new sanctions under the 1988 Act (PCLG, p. 2). By late 1991, 25 councils had had notices issued to them in connection with work covered by the 1980 Act (Department of the Environment, December 1991).

Limited Effect

A survey by the Association of District Councils in 1986 indicated that 73 per cent of them believed that improved value for money had resulted from the 1980 Act (Ivens, 1992, p. 14). However, for years its effects were limited, since authorities were able to circumvent the intention of fair competition. For example, work was arranged so that no outside competitor could realistically tender for it, DLOs were allowed to adjust tender prices in the light of outside bids received, and in some cases DLOs were given work without regard to other bids (Winetrobe, p. 15). In November 1990 The Audit Commission observed that until recently London's building maintenance DLOs (and presumably many elsewhere) found little difficulty in complying with the Local Government, Planning and Land Act 1980 and subsequent regulations. This was because of the 40 per cent competition-free allowance for non-emergency work and the exclusion of work defined as emergencies. Newer regulations have required all building maintenance work to be won in competition (AC90d, sections 85-86).

Direct Labour Organisations

Most local authorities directly employ their own labour to carry out maintenance of municipal buildings, council houses, schools and other educational buildings. A study by the Audit Commission of building maintenance DLOs in London illustrates some of the problems which lack of competition, and council mismanagement, can cause. Audits carried out in 1989-90 in 24 of London's 32 building maintenance DLOs showed that many were subject to low productivity, poor attendance, inadequate supervision, high over-heads, poor quality of service, ineffective client procedures, and weak business management. Inefficient working practices had been allowed to persist in many of the DLOs. Despite low productivity, most operatives achieved bonus earnings at or near maximum levels, since many bonus schemes had very easy targets. Most operatives had shorter working hours and more generous holidays than employees of private contractors, yet sick leave was nearly double that taken by contractors' employees. The excessive absence through claimed sickness is all the more striking in view of one factor for which London DLOs scored well: their health and safety arrangements.

With a few exceptions, standards of supervision were disturbingly low, despite the large number of supervisors—one and a half times the generally accepted norm. Many councils' stores were overstaffed and inefficient, giving a service so poor that it was quicker to bypass them and purchase materials direct. One of the reasons for weak management is that, until comparatively recently, DLO managers tended to be appointed on the basis of length of service in the workforce and with the council. 'The whole culture of some London DLOs has been one of stagnation and lack of responsibility,' stated the Commission, 10 years after the Act which was supposed to make authorities put their DLOs in order (AC90d, summary and sections 13-17, 35-38, 46, 50, 59, 71 and 94). While London's DLOs are probably not representative of local government direct labour departments generally, they illustrate in an acute form the malaise which has long afflicted many of them.

One problem examined in detail by the Audit Commission is absence through sickness. Although particularly severe in London, returns from auditors' work show that DLOs in all types of authority record above-average sickness absence. In a study of 10 London Boroughs as a whole (not just their DLOs), sickness absence cost, in terms of unproductive salaries and wages, on average more than £5 million a year per authority. In the slackest authorities the average amount of sickness absence reached 22 days a year, which is three times national levels (AC90c, sections 3-7 and 10).

The Growth of Competitive Tendering

Competitive tendering and contracting out can take place independently of each other. The majority of competitive tendering for local government services does not result in contracting out, and when contracting out is used it is not always as a result of competitive tendering. Contracting out is sometimes referred to as privatisation, of which in the broad sense of the term it is one form; but it does not usually (and then only incidentally) involve the sale of publicly owned assets. David Parker and Keith Hartley rightly observe that competitive tendering falls far short of complete privatisation since officials still determine what is supplied, and services are still funded out of taxation. Consequently it does not (especially in the absence of bids for alternative levels of service) introduce consumer choice and 'allocative efficiency' (Parker and Hartley, 1990a, p. 12).

A government committee of inquiry, appointed in 1963, looked into the matter of refuse collection and storage and concluded that, in the interests of efficiency and public health, local authorities should not employ contractors to collect household refuse (POP, 1982, p. 18, and Walker & Moore, 1983, p. 15). However, in April 1981 Southend-on-Sea in Essex became the first major council, at least in modern times, to contract out their entire cleaning service. Southend had tried for years to end the wasteful 'task and finish' system in their refuse collection work, and to introduce new working practices for street cleaning. Their failure in this, and the militancy of their workers in the 1979 strike, led the council to put the whole cleaning service up for tender in 1980. Wandsworth in London contracted out street cleaning in February 1982 (Walker & Moore, pp. 15-16). However, by the end of 1981 only three local authorities had private contracts for refuse collection (Domberger, 1986, p. 70).

Limited Interest

Interest in both competitive tendering and contracting out grew slowly during the early 1980s. According to one survey, in the year to March 1985 only about 11 per cent of councils in Britain appeared to have contracted out the provision of any services (39 out of 346 survey respondents). The great majority of councils (about 78 per cent) had neither contracted out any services during the year, *nor considered doing so*; of these, some 39 per cent were Labour-controlled, while about 32 per cent were Conservative (Supplement to *Local Government Chronicle*, 5 July 1985, p. three). The following year 60 councils out of 373 responding (16 per cent) reported contracting services out (Supplement to *Local Government Chronicle*, 4 July 1986, p. nine).

In another survey, it was found in 1984 that 190 local authorities had 'privatised' at least one service; a year later the figure was 200, and in 1987 it had grown to 223 (*Municipal Yearbook*, 1985, 1986 & 1988). However, Kieron Walsh points out:

'The majority of authorities, though, have not taken up competitive tendering on a voluntary basis. Those that have subjected services to competition voluntarily have not normally done so on an extensive basis, and contracts have normally been small' (Walsh, K., 1991, p. 9).

Between 1981 and 1988, however, some 90 formal tenders were issued for refuse collection, street cleaning or associated services. In-house teams retained the work in 49 cases, while the private sector won in 41 cases (McGuirk, 1992, p. 4). The value of local authority work subject to competitive tendering, it was suggested in 1988 (CBI2, pp. 17-18), was unlikely to be more than £400 million—only about 1 per cent of the total of £37,000 million spent by local government in 1987/88.[1] The estimated value of work contracted out in 1987/88, excluding construction and highway maintenance, was only £140 million, most of it being concentrated in a very small number of authorities.

Opposition to Competitive Tendering

Reluctance to change

One of the main consequences of the protected nature of government services is that they frequently fail to be innovative and to seek greater efficiency. Change is troublesome and is more likely to incur penalties if unsuccessful than to bring rewards if successful. Moreover, not making changes is easy and rarely results in penalties. Consequently managers are given little encouragement to prove their innovative abilities and every encouragement to follow precedents and the rule book. Couple these restraints with the problems of an often highly unionised work force with leaders who are suspicious of changes proposed by management, and there is a recipe for continuing stagnation.

In the case of local authorities, where party-political control has become considerably more prevalent in recent decades, there is a further disincentive in the form of conservative politicians (of all political parties) who regard it as normal and natural for various services to be provided by government employees. Many also take a pride in being ultimately in charge of large undertakings, and they see contracting out as taking away the power and control which they have hitherto enjoyed. Pride can play an important part. In Nicholas Ridley's words:

'There is a notion that the more massive the ownership, and the more widespread the provision, the more imposing does the council become and the more central in the eyes of the public. The temptation to municipal aggrandisement is strong' (Ridley, 1988, pp. 26-27).

At a conference in 1988, one participant, Albert Newman, stated:

'It is ... not surprising that the main concern of most members and officers that I have been dealing with is that the defined activities should remain in-house. And this, of course, will tend to preserve the power base of chairmen and individual chief officers' (CP, p. 69).

---

[1] As we shall see later, the amount of local authority work covered by CCT later rose to a proportion some eight times that which prevailed in 1988.

Interventionist Ideals

In the case of socialist politicians particularly, there is a further reluctance to allow any changes if these entail redundancies or loss of earnings or benefits to council workers. Many councils are more anxious to see themselves as model employers than as model suppliers of value-for-money services. Councils and health authorities are employers on a very large scale—in some cities the largest employer is the local authority. Some councils regard one of their major roles as being to provide a form of employment which they can protect, at least to some extent, from the capitalist world outside. They hope also to exercise a degree of 'democratic control' over the local economy, through use of their considerable economic power to induce or compel local business to act in conformity with the council's political wishes. The cause of socialism is still held dear in many local councils, and the municipal field provides an opportunity to maintain the battle against capitalism, irrespective of the political party in power nationally.

Bureaucracy

It would be a mistake, however, to credit socialists with all the opposition to competitive tendering and contracting out. Such is the nature of bureaucracy, whatever party be in control, that it tends to grow if it can, and to fight any attempt to reduce it. Competitive tendering involves the possibility of contracting out, and thus is seen as a threat to the council 'empire'. So there are at least three pressures at work, often in combination, against competitive tendering and the changes which can result from it: conservatism, socialism and bureaucracy. As a result of such pressures, the Government proposals in the consultation paper, *Competition in the Provision of Local Authority Services*, were rejected by all four local authority associations (SGLGA).

Interesting questions arise, as Keith Hartley points out, about the behaviour of decision-makers:

'Are they disinterested individuals selflessly pursuing the interests of the community (whatever these might be)? Or, as officials, are they pursuing their own interests, seeking to maximise the budgets of their departments or their individual income prospects? Or, as politicians, are Ministers using public purchasing to attract votes and win elections? Behaviour will depend upon an individual's employment contract and its reward system' (Hartley, 1991, p. 46).

An analysis of the nature of bureaucracy by two authors in the United States is of interest here. James Bennett and Manuel Johnson look first at what motivates people:

33

'It is tempting to blame the bureaucrat for the problems so common at all levels of government. But public employees as *individuals* are not at fault. When someone goes to work in government, he is not issued a halo, nor does he grow a set of horns. The same is true of those who work in private enterprise: they are inherently neither saints nor sinners. Instead, all people are the same in that they respond to incentives: they seek rewards and avoid punishments. In both the public and the private sector, managers and workers will do things that will increase their salary, position, and prestige and will avoid doing things that will result in pay cuts and demotions.

'The incentives in the public sector and in the private sector are very different. By studying these incentives, it is easy to understand why government so often fails and private firms succeed' (Bennett & Johnson, 1981, p. 20).

They go on to explain that, typically, a bureaucrat does not get rewarded for saving money but does get higher rank, increased salary and greater prestige the more employees he has under him. Thus the incentives for bureaucrats give them an interest in increasing the size and scope of government (Bennett & Johnson, pp. 22-23). We should add that bureaucracy in this sense is far from unknown in the private sector. However, it is in the public sector that it is strongest and most deeply entrenched.

Once new government activities have been instituted, bureaucracy tries to ensure that they continue, even long after the original reason has disappeared and circumstances have radically changed. Few bureaucrats will have an incentive to close the relevant section or department, while many will have a disincentive.

Expressions of Resistance

The reactions of many local authorities and organisations, reflecting their views on the proposals which preceded the main legislation on compulsory competitive tendering (CCT), show not only the pride but also the smugness of these great institutions. The Convention of Scottish Local Authorities expressed these feelings in a classic statement of civic disdain and wounded feelings:

'The Consultation Paper is based on the unjustified and unjustifiable preconceptions that local authorities have neither the competence to obtain, nor interest in securing, value for money in the services which they have a statutory obligation to provide; that the only way of testing value for money is by putting services out to tender against private companies which, irrespective of their lack of experience, are able to provide the equivalent service; and that the Secretary of State is a better judge of value for money for a community than its own elected representatives.

'The government takes no account of the historical tradition of local authorities' dedication and pride in the extent and quality of the provision they make for the people they serve. . . .' (DP, p. 52).

Opposition to the proposed competition came in 1987 from the public works committee of the Association of Metropolitan Authorities, which claimed:

'The government is flying in the face of united opposition from local authorities. We despair at central government's continual meddling in local government affairs. Compulsory competitive tendering has been piloted in the National Health Service—disastrously. Any short term financial gains are far outweighed by the long term disadvantages of this legislation.'

Moreover,

'The Government is undermining local democracy and accountability and eroding local authorities' ability to control directly the services for which they are responsible' (Winetrobe & Nield, p. 7).

Trade Union Opposition

The strongest opposition to both competitive tendering and contracting out has come from trade unions, in particular those for public-sector employees. This has been observed among others by Kate Ascher in Britain (Ascher, 1987, p. 1), by E. S. Savas in the United States (Savas, 1987, p. 257), and by Ed Shann in Australia (Shann, 1990). Minoru Itani in Japan refers to a considerable number of conflicts between local authorities and unions (Itani, 1989, p. 52). Savas notes that contracting is seen as a profound threat by government-employee unions, although he adds that, ironically, the contractor's private employees are themselves often unionised.

The National Union of Public Employees (NUPE) declared that

'The proposals in the Consultation Paper amount to a massive upheaval in local government which threatens the livelihood of hundreds of thousands of dedicated and experienced council staff. . . . At every stage the proposals in the Consultation Paper are biased against quality and public service' (DP, 1988, pp. 52-53).

Rodney Bickerstaffe, NUPE's General Secretary, considered that 'Selling services to the lowest bidder will bring an inevitable decline in services because contractors will only win work by cutting corners'. Moreover, he stated that

'Private contractors cannot provide as good a service as that given by public sector staff whose expertise, loyalty and allegiance, has been built up year after year.'[1]

---

[1] Rodney Bickerstaffe, 'NUPE pledged to defeat evils of privatisation', in Supplement to *Local Government Chronicle*, 5 July 1985, pp. 14-15.

Other opponents of competition include the Trades Union Congress and the Labour Research Department, the latter claiming:

'The "savings" from contracting-out are only achieved at the expense of tens of thousands of jobs, of extremely exploitative pay and conditions, of worse standards of service, of a loss of public accountability, and of increased costs which arise both from contractors' overcharging and from the costs to the state of unemployment. The case for competition has not been made' (PPP, 1987, p. 2).

Further opposition came from the Labour Party. Jack Straw, then Labour spokesman on the environment, said in 1985 that the Conservative Government's proposals were 'a charter for rip-off merchants to make a killing out of the ratepayers. As ever, where persuasion fails with the Government, it uses the jackboot'. Donald Dewar, shadow Scottish Secretary, said in the same year that councils would soon be reduced to the status of 'unwilling and gagged agents of central government, little more than a clearing house for other people's tenders' (Winetrobe, p. 4). However, Ian Holliday observes that

'To place the legislative activity of the Thatcher years in context, it should be noted that much of it would have happened anyway: increased central control of local government dates not from 1979, but from 1974' (Holliday, 1991, p. 59).

Labour Party Proposals

More recently the Labour Party has put forward a number of proposals to improve local government services, with particular emphasis on quality, which it explains means 'reliability, variety and choice for the consumer and partnership with the community'. It would require local authorities to set and publicise targets and standards for each service, and would encourage them to set up a variety of schemes to involve consumer and community groups. The Audit Commission would be transformed into a Quality Commission. The Labour Party proposes to replace the legislation on CCT. It would require an authority to test the effectiveness of services, by inviting alternative provision, only when 'quality audits and re-audits show that services are failing to provide either value for money or value for people' (QS).

The Use of Compulsion

The use of compulsion has had several disadvantages as well as advantages. It has been seen by many councils as interference with the management of local affairs by democratically elected councillors. The Association of District Councils said that 'compulsion is not only unnecessary but counter-productive, and will further undermine democratic accountability for local services' (PPP, p. 5). This has created antagonism, and some councils appear to have reacted by seeking to frustrate the purpose of the legislation as far as possible.[1] Compulsion has also had the effect in some cases of adversely affecting hitherto satisfactory relationships between contractors and councils. In the exaggerated view of Lee Digings, CCT 'with its cut-throat competition has effectively destroyed the basis for constructive relationships between public authorities and the private sector' (Digings, 1991, p. 19). While this has sometimes been a problem, it is likely to be largely a temporary one.

Kate Ascher, in a detailed study, came to the conclusion that

> 'both contracting out and competitive tendering appear to work most smoothly (in terms of both procedures and outputs) in non-political environments. . . . once these techniques are adopted as political rather than as technical solutions, their perceived objectivity disappears and with it goes much of their effectiveness. . . . A second and related conclusion is that both competitive tendering and contracting out are most effective when they arise naturally in response to local needs' (Ascher, 1987, p. 268).

There is some truth in these conclusions, but they disregard the vested interests which prevent the use of competition. They are also much too pessimistic, as the results of CCT have since shown.

Britain appears to be unique in making competitive tendering compulsory for certain local authority services. Competitive tendering is widely used in a number of countries without being compulsory. However, in Britain, by contrast with a number of other countries, very few local authorities voluntarily chose to invite tenders for any of the activities for which they are now obliged to do so, despite evidence that many of them were thereby squandering taxpayers' money. One campaigner for competitive tendering, David Saunders, states that 'the Government found itself, after years of exhortation, driven to compulsion in despair at the failure of Conservative as much as socialist councils to go out to tender voluntarily' (CP, p. 2). As the Audit Commission rightly points out, making competitive tendering compulsory forces 'comparisons between in-house and contractors' costs which authorities ought to have been undertaking as a matter of good management practice'

---

[1] For example, one tactic used by some authorities in relation to vehicle maintenance, as described in *Municipal Journal*, is to bypass the CCT process by selling their fleet of vehicles and entering into leasing arrangements which include maintenance and which are not covered by CCT (Pollard, 1990).

(AC89a, p. 2). Unless there is to be no limit to the extent to which councils may act wastefully with the resources with which they are entrusted, it was concluded that their widespread gross neglect of good management had long been such that finally compulsion was the lesser evil.[1] Councils' attitudes will be explored in more detail later (below, p. 55 *et seq.*).

Directives from the European Community

The organs of the European Economic Community have not omitted to provide their own regulations about public procurement. The Works Directives have for some years applied to the biggest 1980 Act work. As a result of the EEC's Compliance Directive the Government issued new regulations for 'Public Supply Contracts' and 'Public Works Contracts' (PSCR and PWCS) which took effect on 21 December 1991 (*'92 News, Spring 1992*, issued by the AMA). In June 1992 the EEC issued a directive on 'Public Service Contracts' (EC92) with an implementation date of 1 July 1993, which will apply to several types of 1988 Act work. The Chartered Institute of Public Finance and Accountancy has observed that although the purposes of the UK legislation and the EEC's Directives are different, there are marked similarities between them. The two régimes conflict inasmuch as observing both sets of rules simultaneously will for most authorities be more than twice as hard as following either set on its own (ECD, 1991, p. 1).

In a detailed analysis, Lee Digings states that

'practically every local authority contract of any magnitude for works, supplies or services will be subject to complex public procurement rules and procedures emanating from Brussels. ... The extent of regulation is already great and the situation ... will be awesome.' (Digings, 1991, pp. 20-21)

The directives come into effect only when the total value of a contract is above the relevant threshold, such as 200,000 European currency units (ECUs) or about £165,000, but this is not a large amount for an authority in the UK.[2] Although the

---

1 Robin Wendt, of the Association of County Councils, points out that central government funds 85 per cent of local government, entitling them to impose measures of CCT. He adds: 'This is an issue we can't ignore—if we hold our begging bowl out too often we can't complain if we get our fingers chopped' (Burton, 1992b, pp. 14-15).

2 The Association of Metropolitan Authorities (AMA) have pointed out that since the threshold of 200,000 ECU, above which the EC Directive applies, refers to the total value of a contract, not its annual value, a six-year contract worth about £22,000 a year would be subject to the procedures. Thus they add: 'a contract for the cleaning of a secondary school in Sheffield may have to be advertised all over the EC!' (AMA, p. 3).

regulations are formally impartial, contracting authorities in the United Kingdom are expected to bear a heavier administrative burden than those elsewhere because of their larger size. For example, in England over 99 per cent of municipalities have a population of over 10,000, whereas in France about 2½ per cent are that large, and in Germany about 14 per cent. The likely consequence of these added regulations is more bureaucracy, particularly for the UK, without any tangible benefits.[1] Moreover, the interplay of CCT and the Services Directive will, Digings states, see UK authorities caught in a double bureaucracy (Digings, 1991, pp. 20-21, 23 and 35-37).

---

[1] The AMA stated, in response to the EC Services Directive at its proposal stage, that a DSO, having won a contract under both the 1988 Act and the EC's Directive, could then be subject again to the requirements of this or other procurement directives, for example to obtain supplies. Such requirements would not apply to a private contractor, and would mean DSOs being subjected to unfair additional costs (AMA, p. 1).

THREE

The Local Government Act 1988

In this chapter we examine the 1988 Act's requirements, the savings expected to result (savings achieved in practice are examined in the next chapter), the element of compulsion, the danger of monopolies, and the fairness of the legislation. Thereafter the attitudes of councils and of contractors are considered, as are the question of service specifications, the interests of voluntary organisations, ways in which competition could usefully be widened, and government proposals for reform and extension of the law.

Requirements of the Act

In February 1985 the Government published a consultative paper on *Competition in the Provision of Local Authority Services*, but legislation was slow to follow. The Queen's Speech in November 1986 included an intention to introduce legislation, and in June 1987 there followed a Bill resulting in the Local Government Act 1988 which received the Royal Assent on 24 March 1988.

The Act obliges 'defined authorities'—local authorities, and certain other public bodies,[1] in Britain (but not in Northern Ireland)—to invite tenders for what is called 'functional work' for the provision of services in certain areas of activity.[2] Initially, the

---

[1] The defined authorities to which Part 1 of the Act applies are as follows (LGA, Part 1, section 1, and CH, 1992, pp. 4-5): local authorities; urban development corporations such as those established for London Docklands and Cardiff Bay; development corporations for new towns; the Commission for the New Towns; police and fire authorities including the London Fire and Civil Defence Authority; metropolitan county passenger transport authorities; waste disposal authorities such as the London Waste Regulation Authority and the Merseyside Waste Disposal Authority; joint education committees; water development boards in Scotland; the Scottish Special Housing Association.

Where two or more defined authorities arrange, under section 101 of the Local Government Act 1972, for the discharge by a joint committee of theirs of any of their functions, the committee itself is treated as a defined authority as regards the application of CCT to England and Wales.

[2] Functional work is defined negatively, in that it is (principally) work carried out by a defined authority, other than work carried out under a 'works contract'. Works contract means a contract constituting or including an agreement which provides

[*Cont'd. on p. 41*]

areas of activity for which tenders are required were: collection of refuse; cleaning of buildings; other cleaning; catering for purposes of schools and welfare; other catering; maintenance of ground; and repair and maintenance of vehicles (LGA, section 2).[1] Where work is concerned with more than one of the defined activities (such as the maintenance of vehicles for refuse collection), an authority can decide in which activity to include it. Work which is not covered by the legislation can be included with work which is covered where to do so suits the authority.

---

for the carrying out of work by a defined authority. Work which is incidental or preparatory to functional work as just defined, but which is carried out by another organisation by sub-contract, is also functional work. Functional work is in most instances work done for an authority by its own works department; but it includes also work carried out on an agency basis for another authority. The main requirements for competitive tendering apply to functional work. The situation differs in the case of works contracts, where an authority contracts (otherwise than under an agency arrangement) for the provision of work, usually with another authority. In this case the Act imposes just two conditions if the work falls within a defined activity. These conditions are, briefly, (1) either that the work is done in response to an invitation also made to at least three other appropriate persons who are not themselves defined authorities, or that invitations to submit offers to do the work were published in at least one local newspaper and one trade journal, and (2) that the client does not act in a manner having the effect, or intended or likely to have the effect of restricting, distorting or preventing competition (CCTLGA, 1991, pp. 15-16).

[1] The 'collection of refuse' applies to both household and commercial (but not industrial) waste. The 'cleaning of buildings' refers to windows on both sides and the interiors of buildings, including the common areas of blocks of flats. Dwellings, residential establishments (including old people's homes and children's homes) and police buildings are excluded. 'Other cleaning' means the cleaning of streets including removal of litter (from any land, not just streets), emptying of litter bins, sweeping, emptying of gullies, and the cleaning of traffic signs and street name plates; it does not include clearing of snow as this is considered to be an 'emergency' activity and thus exempt. Catering for schools includes everything from provision of ingredients to serving the meals, as well as providing refreshments for consumption in schools. In residential homes and day centres it includes preparation but not serving of meals. However, residential schools, special schools, residential homes and day centres in which meals are prepared on the premises are excluded. The preparation of meals on wheels is included, but not their delivery. 'Other catering' is similar to that for schools but refers to staff canteens, leisure centres and the like; however, catering in institutions of further education is excluded. In the view of the Department of the Environment, providing refreshments includes the running of licensed bars. 'Maintenance of ground' includes grass cutting and tending (including re-turfing and re-seeding), planting and tending of trees, hedges, shrubs, flowers and other plants, and control of weeds. Landscaping, and initial turfing and seeding, are excluded, as is any activity if its primary purpose is research or securing the survival of any kind of plant. 'Repair and maintenance of vehicles' includes any motor vehicle or trailer but excludes repair of damage caused by an accident, and excludes police vehicles. A subsequent Order by the Secretary of State exempted the maintenance of all vehicles used, by defined authorities, solely in connection with the discharge of their functions as fire authorities (LGA, Schedule 1, and LGAC, 1988, paras. 5-12).

The Secretary of State may provide by order, made by statutory instrument (subject to approval by Parliament), for the exclusion of any of these 'defined activities', or for the addition of an activity. One activity, management of sport and leisure facilities, was added in December 1989. The 1988 Act also added one activity—the maintenance of street lighting—to those covered by the 1980 Act: construction, repair and maintenance of buildings, and maintenance of sewers.

DLOs and DSOs

The Local Government, Planning and Land Act 1980 required certain building, construction and maintenance work to be exposed to competition, and led local authorities to create, for accounting purposes, separate Direct Labour Organisations (DLOs) as internal contracting arms, and referred to them as such. Similarly, the 1988 Act gave rise to the creation of Direct Service Organisations (DSOs) along the same lines. The difference between DLOs and DSOs is mainly one of name, and of the legislation in response to which they were created. The 1988 Act itself refers to a 'direct labour organisation or a similar organisation', but a subsequent circular from the Department of the Environment concerning that Act refers to the in-house organisations as DSOs (LGAC, 1988, para. 2).

Applicability

The 1988 Act applies when any of the defined activities are carried out by an authority's own staff, or by a company associated with an authority—that is, a company whose members include the authority or any of its members or officers, or any holding company or subsidiary of such a company. The Act allows local authorities to use their own staff to provide the defined services only if they have won a contract to do so in competition with outside businesses. Separate internal accounts must be kept for any of these services which are supplied by local authority staff, and annual financial reports prepared for them. When inviting tenders, authorities must do so from at least three private contractors, or as many as wish to bid if the number wishing to do so is less than three. Other authorities' DSOs may also be invited to bid, but such invitations must be in addition to, and not in place of, the minimum number of private bids.[1]

---

[1] The Secretary of State may by regulations vary the minimum number of 'persons' who have to be invited to bid, and the minimum number who must be private contractors. The Department of the Environment, in a circular on anti-competitive

[Cont'd. on p. 43]

The CCT provisions of the 1988 Act apply only if an authority wishes to give work to its own, or another authority's, DSO. Consequently, if a council decides to employ an outside contractor it is not obliged to use competitive tendering. Indeed, the Audit Commission has observed that

'There are examples of authorities which are operating a 100 per cent contracting out policy but are not maximising their value for money because they use a restricted list of contractors or award contracts without competitive tendering' (AC89a, p. 3).

There are several grounds for exclusion from these rules. When the work relates to an emergency or disaster (actual or potential), or when it is a minor part of the job of someone whose main work is not one of the defined activities, the provisions of the Act do not apply. The *'de minimis'* rule, made by Order of the Secretary of State, excludes defined activities where the estimated gross cost of work carried out by the authority itself does not exceed £100,000 a year.[1]

Phased Introduction

Not all the defined activities were made subject to CCT at one time. Partly to give authorities time to prepare for the changes, and partly so as not to overwhelm private contractors, the Act provided for a phased introduction of CCT, the details of which were provided in statutory instruments. For most services, authorities were put into groups, with different groups having different timetables in respect of which services had to be put out to tender by particular dates.[2]

---

behaviour in May 1991, indicated that it could be anti-competitive to restrict invitations to three where more potentially suitable tenderers have asked to be invited. There is reference to four to six tenders being appropriate, although there is no legal basis for this (CCTLGA, p. 10). Although the term 'Secretary of State' is used throughout the 1988 Act in accordance with convention, the Secretary of State for Scotland exercises in relation to Scottish authorities those powers given under the Act to the Secretary of State.

[1] This figure applies to the whole of an authority's expenditure in carrying out each defined activity in-house. The Order also excludes from compulsory competition the work of employees, such as residential caretakers in schools, who are required as a condition of their employment to live in particular accommodation for the better performance of their duties (LGAC, paras. 17-18). Exemption from CCT of elements of a defined activity, although generally welcomed by local authorities, sometimes causes problems, as in the case of 'dual-use' sports facilities ('Troubled waters still not clear', *Local Government Chronicle*, 6 September 1991, p. 26).

[2] For these services there was a three-year period for bringing in CCT, which started on 1 August 1989. Each group of authorities was assigned a different sequence for the activities which they had to put out to tender, with fresh deadlines at six-monthly intervals. However, the Department of the Environment's 'litter code' of 1990 had the effect of delaying for one round all work under the heading 'other cleaning' which had not already been put to tender.

Ground maintenance was treated differently, in that a minimum of 20 per cent of total expenditure had to be put out to tender each year cumulatively over five years, starting on 1 January 1990. For management of sport and leisure facilities, the timetable is based on gross expenditure, with 35 per cent subject to CCT by January 1992, 70 per cent by August 1992, and 100 per cent by January 1993.

Contract Periods

Following the passing of the Act, the Secretary of State issued a consultation paper on contract periods and then decided to set minimum and maximum periods. Minima are 3, 4 or 5 years, while maxima are 4, 5, 6 or 7 years, depending on the activity and on whether or not an authority has education functions.[1] Authorities are obliged to make specifications available for inspection free of charge, and to supply copies for a reasonable charge.[2]

Non-Commercial Matters

The Act attempts to prevent authorities from taking into account any of a number of 'non-commercial matters' in the course of tendering procedures. It specifically prohibits councils from introducing any of various considerations in drawing up contracts, inviting tenders or making or terminating contracts.[3] This

---

[1] Shorter minima and maxima were set for education authorities' building cleaning and ground maintenance, and a shorter maximum for school and welfare catering, in order to hasten the transition to full budget delegation under the Education Reform Act (LGAC, paras. 38-39).

[2] The term 'reasonable' is not defined, but the Secretary of State has expressed the view that, since authorities are under a statutory duty to draw up the specification, they should not reflect the cost of doing so in the charge made for copies. The charge should, therefore, reflect no more than the marginal cost of producing and supplying an extra copy (LGAC, para. 30).

[3] These considerations are:

o Terms and conditions of employment, composition of the workforce, promotion and training policies, etc.;

o The use, if any, of self-employed labour;

o Any involvement of the business activities or interests of contractors with irrelevant fields of government policy (such as defence);

o The conduct of contractors in industrial disputes;

o The country of origin of supplies to contractors or the location of contractors' business links (for example, South Africa);

o Any political, industrial or sectarian affiliations or interests of contractors or their directors, partners or employees (such as with freemasonry);

o Financial support or lack of support by contractors for any institution to or from which the authority gives or withholds support;

o Use or non-use by contractors of technical or professional services provided by the authority under certain Acts (LGA, section 17, and IDS, 1988, pp. 20-21).

[*Cont'd. on p. 45*]

prohibition applies to all the defined authorities' public supply and works contracts, and not only to those subject to CCT (CTCC, 1988, p. 14).

Where a contractor believes that an authority has applied impermissible non-commercial criteria in refusing a contract, he can seek a judicial review and sue for damages if the complaint is upheld. Where a contractor has been turned down by a local authority, or excluded from an approved list, the authority is obliged to provide on request written reasons for the decision (IDS, 1988, p. 21). A condition of compliance with the Act is that authorities do not act 'in a manner having the effect or intended or likely to have the effect of restricting, distorting or preventing competition'.[1]

Accounting Requirements

The Secretary of State has specified that authorities carrying out defined activities are required to produce a 5 per cent rate of return on current valued net assets (the same target as for construction and maintenance work subject to Part III of the 1980 Act) for most defined activities. The exceptions are building cleaning, the management of sport and leisure facilities, and any other activity for which it has been made clear that the capital employed by the authority would be made available to whoever might be awarded the work; in these cases, because they require very little if any

---

An exception is explicitly made for one non-commercial matter: authorities may ask 'approved questions' in writing of contractors concerning their workforces and policies in respect of racial discrimination, and may include terms or provisions in draft contracts to secure compliance with section 71 of the Race Relations Act 1976 (LGA, section 18, and IDS, p. 21). The permitted questions exclude, however, any reference to 'ethnic monitoring', and this has been described by the chairman of the Commission for Racial Equality as a serious omission (IDS, p. 21). The approved questions are those specified by the Secretary of State (CTCC, pp. 19-20). However, similar questions are not allowed in connection with sex or disablement. Reasonable inquiries about contractors' health and safety records and arrangements, and about the qualifications of a contractor's workforce, are permissible. Employment of disabled persons and apprentices and trainees are also matters which can be taken into account, as permitted under the 1980 Act (Parker, 1990b, p. 662). The Secretary of State, with the approval of Parliament, can amend the existing definitions of non-commercial matters, and can specify other matters as non-commercial (CTCC, p. 15).

[1] Anti-competitive behaviour is not easy to define exhaustively, and the Act does not attempt to provide such a definition. However, the Secretary of State has stated that behaviour likely to be regarded as anti-competitive includes the following: making contracts too large for contractors to compete for; giving contractors too little time to respond to tender invitations; seeking detailed and sensitive information about companies which goes beyond that needed to assess their ability to carry out work properly; requiring contractors to provide excessive performance bonds; and, of course, rejecting lower tenders from contractors in favour of the DSO's bid without good reason (LGAC, para. 33).

capital to be supplied by the contractor, the objective is that revenue in any financial year be not less than expenditure (LGAC, para. 42 and Annex A; LGAFO, 1991).

The Act requires authorities to keep separate accounts, with some exceptions, for each financial year for each defined activity carried out by a DSO. Authorities must also prepare annual DSO reports for any financial years in which competition applies, and these must be sent to the Secretary of State and to the authority's auditor, and be made accessible to the public. The Secretary of State has powers to specify what items are to be included in DSOs' accounts.

The legislation is not precise on the question of what costs can be taken into account when comparing in-house with outside tenders.[1] However, the Secretary of State's view is that additional costs incurred as a result of employing disabled people, apprentices or trainees, or of providing places on government-sponsored training schemes, may be taken into account (i.e. omitted). Adding costs for extra supervision to outside contractors' bids is not considered legitimate unless there is 'specific quantified evidence' that higher costs will be necessary, since a supervisory structure should be required in any event (CCTLGA, 1991, pp. 28-30).

There is nothing in the legislation requiring an authority to accept the lowest tender it receives, nor would this be expected in every case. If, however, an authority rejects a private contractor's bid in favour of a higher one from its DSO, then the onus will be on the authority to demonstrate that this was done for sound reasons and not in a manner having the effect, or intended or likely to have the effect, of restricting, distorting or preventing competition.

Expected Savings

Audit Commission Findings

In 1987 the Audit Commission published the results of its examination of three services where there was experience of

---

[1] One contentious issue has been the extent to which authorities may legitimately take account of the potential costs of making DSO staff redundant when assessing the overall cost of accepting a contractor's bid, and therefore in deciding whether to keep work in-house. The Secretary of State has stated that the comparison of bids should be made on the basis of spreading the cost of redundancies over the length of the contract. Authorities were advised in 1988 that they should not use redundancy costs again in a second round of competition to justify rejection of lower tenders, as this practice could be regarded as anti-competitive (LGAC, paras. 34-35). Later this view was modified: authorities were told that prospective redundancy costs could be taken into account each time tenders are invited and compared, so long as proper account of the cumulative effect of this is taken, and weighed against the cumulative effect of potential savings from otherwise lower bids forgone (CCTLGA, 1991, p. 29).

46

competition between DLOs and private-sector suppliers: refuse collection, vehicle maintenance, and repairs and improvements to council houses. It stated that in each case the evidence is irrefutable that:

o Costs incurred are higher if services are not subject to competition.

o Major cost savings would result if all local authorities were able to obtain services at the costs already secured by the most successful 25 per cent of authorities.

o The most competitive DLOs have costs that are lower than the prices quoted by the average suppliers; but an average DLO's costs are higher than those of private suppliers[1]—that is, most DLOs are not fully cost-competitive (AC87, p. 2).

The potential savings if all authorities matched the performance of the better ones (the first quartile in terms of cost) were estimated by the Audit Commission for three services as follows: house maintenance—20 per cent; vehicle management—25 per cent; refuse collection—15 per cent.

In 1988 the Audit Commission examined the management of parks and green spaces, on which councils in England and Wales spend about £780 million a year. Gross savings from competition were expected, on the basis of limited but clear experience, to be between 10 and 30 per cent, and in the authorities on which these figures are based there is no evidence to suggest that there has been any decline in standards. The one-off client-side cost of setting up a contract is about 4-6 per cent of the annual contract sum, and annual costs of administration and supervision (much of which should be incurred already) were put at about 4 per cent. Consequently, net savings were expected to be in the range of 5-25 per cent a year (AC88b, pp. 4, 31 and 33).

Academic Surveys

A study in 1986 of the effect of competitive tendering for refuse collection, found that costs were lower by about 22 per cent

---

[1] For example, the Audit Commission stated that in a survey on the maintenance of council houses it found that the cost of re-wiring per dwelling varied between £218 and £396 for private contractors, but the cost for work not subject to competition averaged about £600. One DLO was charging over £2,000 per dwelling for roof tiling, compared with £800 to £1,200 for similar work let on a competitive contract in a nearby authority (AC87, p. 2). According to the Commission for Local Authority Accounts in Scotland, education authorities in Scotland could save 20 per cent on janitorial (caretaking) and cleaning bills by eliminating inefficient working practices (*Public Service Review*, No. 16, p. 4).

where private contracting took place. Even where tenders were awarded in-house, costs were lower by about 17 per cent. The authors of the survey, S. Domberger, S. A. Meadowcroft and D. J. Thompson, conclude therefore that it is the introduction of competition, rather than awarding of contracts to private firms, which is the crucial factor in achieving lower costs. Few authorities where competition is absent matched the efficiency of those where tendering had been introduced, and the vast majority were less efficient than private contractors. The analysis took into account the two main aspects of service quality—method and frequency of collection. Savings from tendering increased from 12 per cent in the first year to 25 per cent in later years, suggesting that there were significant transitional costs in the first year of adopting competition, but that these did not last long. The findings indicate that if all the relevant authorities in England and Wales (rather than only 38 out of 403) had tendered their refuse services in 1984/85, costs would have been cut by £80 million (Domberger, 1986). These results were challenged by Joe Ganley and John Grahl who suggested that the cost reductions were overestimated and important losses were ignored (Ganley and Grahl, 1988). Domberger *et al.* replied to these criticisms, and referred to other evidence that was consistent with their findings (Domberger, 1988).

Further analysis by John Cubbin, Simon Domberger and Shirley Meadowcroft indicates that the major part of the savings produced by private contractors was due to improved technical efficiency (on average 17 per cent out of 22 per cent), while for in-house savings less than a half were due to increased technical efficiency (an average of 7 per cent out of 17 per cent). The authors point out that their results do not support the view of some commentators who have asserted that savings are largely the result of lower wages and fringe benefits for the employees concerned. Besides technical efficiency, other possible sources of savings are changes in the vehicle-labour mix and reductions in overheads (Cubbin, 1987).

Competition

Domberger *et al.*'s conclusion supports that of Robert Poole who found that

'In empirical studies comparing the costs of public services, the most important factor generally is *not* whether the providers are public or private but whether the service is provided under competitive or monopolistic conditions' (Poole, 1983).

It seems reasonable to interpret this as implying that, if private-sector organisations are usually more efficient than those in the public sector, it is mainly because it is less usual for private organisations to be protected from competition. It is not contracting out as such but rather competition which improves efficiency.

The size of the municipal cleansing market alone (refuse collection and street cleaning) is large, with 454 authorities putting out to tender work worth over £700 million between August 1989 and January 1992. On average over 180 contracts are coming up for tender each year (RC, p. 5). The annual value of work subject to competition under the 1980 and 1988 Acts together has been estimated at about £5,000 million, so the scope for efficiency savings is large (COLG, 1988, p. 32).

The Danger of Monopolies and Cartels

The Audit Commission points out that

> 'Privatisation will not necessarily secure competitiveness. . . . privatising a service in total could result in replacement of a public monopoly with a private one, unless authorities retain an in-house capability to ensure that contractors remain cost competitive' (AC87, p. 4).

This is a possibility in certain circumstances. The risk is, however, likely to diminish as contracting out becomes more widespread since there are then likely to be more private contractors able and willing to do the kinds of work required by local authorities. A Treasury-sponsored report on using private enterprise in government states: 'Intelligent purchasing will involve keeping competition alive by sharing contracts among firms and encouraging new firms to enter the industry' (HMT, 1986, p. 35).

Joe Painter sees a risk of what he calls 'centralisation of capital' associated in particular with multinational companies. There are, he points out, considerable differences in this respect between the various services. In contract catering, for example, three companies, Gardner Merchant, Sutcliffe Catering Group and Compass Services account for 60 per cent of the market. By contrast, the grounds maintenance sector is made up of a profusion of small and medium-sized firms (Painter, 1990, p. 20).

Cartels are a related danger mentioned by Michael Willson who considers that

> 'The cut and thrust of entrepreneurial life is a fine place to visit but no-one in their right mind actually wants to live there. Commercial life is full of examples of how we seek to protect ourselves from the uncertainty and short-term horizons of free markets.'

He adds more specifically that 'What we know is that the major players, with most experience of contracting, always gravitate to cartel arrangements' (Willson, 1991, p. 3).

Similarly, Keith Hartley and Meg Huby state that, while those in private industry stress the benefits of free enterprise and competition,

'in reality, businessmen have long shown a remarkable propensity for seeking monopoly, protection and government subsidies leading to on-the-job leisure and a quiet life' (Hartley, 1985, p. 23).

This is not new. Adam Smith observed that

'People of the same trade seldom meet together, even for merriment and diversion, but the conversation ends in a conspiracy against the public, or in some contrivance to raise prices'.[1]

This danger may be exaggerated, but it must be guarded against, and nowadays there is much legislation for the purpose. In the present context, Hartley and Huby stress that the results of competitions should be publicly available, and that details of the winning and rival bids should be published. Publication reduces the danger of political patronage in the award of contracts, and the information also contributes to the competitive process: winners and losers need to know how they compare (Hartley, 1985, p. 25).

The ways in which the actions of government have, both intentionally and inadvertently, promoted a reduction in competition in many fields is beyond the scope of the present study. In this context, however, an example might be provided by the large size of many contracts which is probably a factor encouraging firms to merge. Authorities which sought to exclude competition by, for example, combining all their refuse collection and street cleaning requirements into a single contract may be responsible for the growth of correspondingly large contractors partly through the expansion into Britain of large French and Spanish companies (see McGuirk, 1992, pp. 6-7).

Survey of Private Tenderers

A survey of 3,475 local authority contracts in England and Wales by the Local Government Management Board lists the major successful private tenderers and, for contracts where values are known (that is, for the great majority), the proportions of the different types of work which they have won. For example, in building cleaning more than 32 companies (or groups of companies with common ownership) shared the work not won by DSOs, with no one company or group of companies having more than about

---

[1] Adam Smith, *The Wealth of Nations*, Book I, Chap.10, Everyman edition, London: J. M. Dent, 1975.

Table 1:
**Numbers of Contracts and Share of Contracts Won
for Local Government Services, 1988-1991***

Service	(A) Number	(B) £000 p.a.	(C) %	(D) %
Building cleaning	>32	430	2·5	17
Refuse collection	19	1,373	4·3	18
Refuse collection and other cleaning combined	10	1,939	3·4	18
Other cleaning	>18	476	4·6	27
Vehicle maintenance	>12	461	2·7	21
Catering (education and welfare)	>5	1,864	2·3	. . .
Catering (other)	>13	155	2·6	15
Ground maintenance	>15	296	5·1	29
Sport and leisure management	>3	605	. . .	. . .

. . . = not available or not applicable.

*The period covered is from the implementation of the 1988 Act up to publication of CCTIS (April 1991).

Source: CCTIS (1991), pp. 12-13, 19, 24, 26, 32, 38, 42, 50 & 56.

2·5 per cent by value of the total business, or about 17 per cent of the amount won by private contractors. Comparing this with other services produces the results shown in Table 1, where (A) is the number of company groups based on those named, (B) is the average size of all contracts (in-house and other) on an annual basis, (C) is the largest percentage (by value) of all contracts won by a single private contractor or group, and (D) is the largest percentage (again, by value) won by a private contractor, of all contracts won by private contractors.[1] The figures for refuse collection include those for contracts where refuse collection and other cleaning have been combined. The Table shows that the proportion of work in each activity won by the largest private contracting group in the sector varies between 2½ and 5 per cent of the total for the

---

[1] The percentages are approximate, partly because they are based on incomplete coverage, and partly because of the way in which they are derived from the published tables. The number of private businesses winning contracts, given in column (A), is a minimum in the case of activities for which the source table does not name them all. In the case of sports and leisure management, meaningful annual figures are available for only about half the contracts.

activity, and from 15 to 29 per cent of the work in the activity won by all private contractors. There are various factors which lead to differing degrees of concentration in different sectors, some of them inherent in the nature of the business but others of which are artificial and often the consequence of government decisions. One important factor, discussed later (below, pp. 97-99), may be the size of contracts.

The Audit Commission has observed that, while there is a well-established private sector in services such as building cleaning, vehicle maintenance and catering, the markets for ground maintenance, refuse collection and street cleaning will have to expand markedly if all authorities are to be presented with a genuine choice of contractor (AC89a, p. 15). However, the relative absence of private contractors for tasks which have traditionally been kept in-house by local authorities is not surprising in the case of activities, such as street cleaning, for which there can be little demand (in the economic sense) except from such authorities. The requirement under the 1988 Act to invite bids from a minimum of (only) three private contractors for work subject to CCT has been criticised. In so far as restricting the bidding limits competition, raises costs and increases the risk of collusion and corruption, this provision is described as unfortunate (Parker, 1990b, p. 662). But more important at present is evidently the problem of getting even as many as three contractors to tender for some of the services in question in some areas of Britain. The extent of competition for local authority contracts is discussed later (below, pp. 73-76).

Is the Legislation Fair?

Financial Targets

On both sides—that of the council's workforce and that of the contractors—there are complaints that the legislation is unfair. There are also complaints that the implementation of the legislation by particular councils is unfair. The 1988 Act requires authorities to set up separate trading accounts for the relevant services, and for in-house suppliers to meet minimal financial targets specified by the Secretary of State. Where little or no capital is required, the target is to break even, while in all other cases the target is a return on capital of 5 per cent. This is to compensate for the fact that a DSO does not have to raise capital in the same way as a private company. It is objected that this is unfair since, as outside contractors have no such compulsory targets, they can undercut local authorities by reducing their profit margins, at least for a period (Painter, 1990, p. 5). There is some truth in this allegation[1] but David Thompson has explained:

> 'A loss-leading strategy is one that is workable only for the sorts of services where some special-product expertise is relevant. Loss-leading is a worthwhile strategy only if you are able to secure the market and then put in a bid above the competitive level and *still* win the contract. It seems to me that for a basic service like refuse collection, the expectations of being able to bid above the market level second time around and still win the contract are very low. I would not expect loss-leading to be effective' (TT, 1990, p. 41).

The Audit Commission has objected to the target of 5 per cent return on capital employed, partly because 'balance sheets are always liable to manipulation to reduce recorded capital employed artificially'. Furthermore, 'a private sector contractor can bid on a "marginal" basis simply to contribute to his fixed overheads. This flexibility should be available to the DLO' (AC87, p. 7). On the other hand, it has been objected that the 5 per cent target is a modest one, and that many managers in the private sector would be very happy with having to make only a 5 per cent rate of return on their capital, particularly in view of the rates of interest they have often had to pay to get the capital (TT, p. 47).

Perceived Problems

Writing on behalf of contractors, John Hall a few years ago expressed the view that many companies in a wide range of industries were reassessing their attitude to public-sector work, much of which was perceived to be unprofitable, high-risk work relevant only to the very largest companies, able to take the long-term view of a return on their investment in the tendering process. He argued that contractors are disadvantaged by the need to take into account the cost to them of redundancies arising from subsequent loss of a contract (Hall, pp. 1 & 5). Councils are allowed to take into account the cost of making their own employees redundant when comparing DSO and outside contractors' bids, and to spread this cost over the period of the contract.[2] It has been argued that this is a one-off transfer of a liability and should be

---

[1] Lesley Courcouf of the Association of Metropolitan Authorities, claims that reports of loss-leading bids are becoming more common as the recession hits the private sector and firms are desperate for local authority work to survive. One example given is that of private building contractors bidding for councils' ground maintenance work to keep in business (Courcouf, 1991).

[2] It is said that, in order to compete in the NHS, contractors' prices had to beat direct labour by at least 15 per cent to offset in-house redundancy costs added to contractors' bids before prices were compared (SITH, p. 4).

amortised over a long period. For example, when cleaning was contracted out at the Ministry of Defence, redundancy costs were spread over 20 years (TT, p. 46). In central government a minimum of 10 years is recommended (MTBI, 1992, p. 18) for allocation of redundancy costs, whereas in local government and the NHS shorter periods appear to be widely used. This matter ought to be re-examined.

Although a stated aim of the 1988 Act was 'to secure that local and other public bodies undertake certain activities only if they can do so competitively', there is in fact no compulsion to buy services competitively from an outside contractor. It is argued that this gives a bias in favour of the private sector,

> 'since the time-consuming and costly tendering procedure is only required if the council wishes to try to retain services in-house. If the council decides simply to privatise a service, then it does not have to engage in competition at all' (Painter, 1990, p. 4).

This is so, although in practice very few councils, even among those which are the most active in contracting out, appear to avoid CCT in this way. Nevertheless, competition should be the rule in all cases.

Evidence has been put forward that the *de minimis* exemption level of £100,000 is too low. It is said that for many small authorities, particularly in Scotland, costs outweigh any savings or prospect of savings. This is largely because of the dearth of competition; in Scotland in the first 18 months of CCT more than half of all contracts put out to tender did not attract a single bid. Examples from various small authorities appear to demonstrate the problem (Burton, 1992c). An impartial investigation is called for, to see whether the exemption level should be changed.

Restrictions on DSOs

Under the Local Authorities (Goods and Services) Act 1970, DSOs can tender for and carry out 'cross-boundary' work for authorities other than those by which they are employed, and for other public bodies, but not for the private sector. Some argue that this unfairly restricts their ability to compete with private contractors which are not subject to such a limitation. The Audit Commission, which incidentally states that some DSOs are 'sailing close to the wind in extending the range of organisations they work for', points out that

> 'DSOs are not private companies and would not be taking the same risks in the market place. They would not become bankrupt if they failed; instead the ratepayer would meet the bill' (AC89a, p. 22).

In a sense it is unfair that DSOs may not compete freely, but equally it would be unfair if they were allowed to use and risk taxpayers' money in competition with tax-paying private businesses. One solution is for those workers and managers who wish to be free to compete on equal terms, to do so by setting up or buying out their own business and operating in their own right.

In some cases DSOs have been invited, by private contractors putting in bids, to act as their sub-contractors, but this form of co-operation is apparently not permitted. As expressed by a representative of one county council:

'A combination where we can carry out part of the work very efficiently and they can carry out part of the work very efficiently seems sensible: but we are stopped from doing so within the same contract. We cannot act as a sub-contractor doing our own work' (TT, 1990, pp. 14-15).

This appears to be an unreasonable restriction.

The Attitudes of Councils

While a few councils have been enthusiastic about competitive tendering, many have been hostile both to CCT in particular and to competitive tendering in general, as well as to the possibility of contracting out. Of a panel of 40 authorities surveyed by INLOGOV, none had a positive desire to see work done in the private sector, 12 were neutral, 10 preferred to see the DSO win, and 18 adopted an attitude of greater or lesser hostility to competition and favouring the DSO in so far as they could (Walsh, K., 1991, pp. 16-18).

On the other hand, *The Economist*, after remarking that DSOs have become more efficient, has claimed:

'The main catalyst for this improved efficiency has been the mere prospect of tendering. It has given many councils a welcome pretext for taking on their union-dominated workforces. Many Labour councils, in particular, have long been desperate for an excuse to take on their supposed political allies in the local-authority trade unions' (*The Economist*, 9 September 1989, p. 36).

However, according to a survey published in January 1990, 35 per cent of Conservative, 34 per cent of Liberal Democrat but only 12 per cent of Labour councils had awarded contracts to the private sector (Holliday, 1991, p. 52).

Few councils have welcomed competitive tendering whole-heartedly. Among them are the London boroughs of Bromley, Wandsworth and Westminster. Bromley has contracted out at least a dozen services; more than 20 contractors are involved, and average savings are put at around 15 per cent. The story of Wandsworth's achievements has been told elsewhere (Beresford, 1987). Westminster describes itself as the most advanced in the UK for competitive tendering, and has contracted out 23 services with 36 contracts, of which seven were chosen on grounds of quality and not simply cost (Burton, 1992b).

Several cities in North America have used both public and private refuse collection services in different areas, allowing comparison of the results in practice, and encouraging improvements (Rehfuss, 1989, pp. 45 & 54; David, 1988, p. 47). Even this cautious yet progressive approach does not appear to have been widely adopted in Britain. Clearly one reason why many councils seek to protect their DSOs is that many of them see the DSOs' purpose as being not just to provide services but also to serve as means whereby they can pursue political objectives, particularly in employment practices. The Audit Commission has observed that it is 'aware of a wide range of strategies adopted by authorities to avoid tackling the problems of non-competitive in-house services' (AC87, p. 7). Joe Painter has pointed out that

'the way in which competitive tendering legislation works out on the ground, as it were, can vary very significantly depending on the political attitude of the authority, as well as on trade union activity and the level of private sector competition' (Painter, 1990, p. 17).

If a local authority seeks to get the best value from competitive tendering, the sensible course is for it to consult both its DSO and appropriate contractors on the size and packaging of proposed contracts. Yet out of 40 authorities questioned by INLOGOV, only two said they had explicitly consulted contractors, and most felt that this was an improper practice. How many had consulted their DSOs, or felt it improper to do so, is not stated (Walsh, K., 1991, p. 13).

Obstructing Competition

Richard Kerley and Douglas Wynn comment that in Scotland:

'Instead of dealing with willing clients for their cleansing or catering services, private contractors were faced with public bodies which, in general, resented their approaches and did what they could within the law to see that they were unsuccessful in tendering'.

Most council members and staff do not see their only or even primary function as being the provision of services to the public, since they are more concerned with providing jobs.

'Thus for many members it appears that the intellectual and emotional challenge first raised through the prospect of discussing the tendering of defined activities is exactly as it is for staff. That is, actually having to consider the prospect of services customarily, even unthinkingly, being done by directly employed staff now possibly being done by contractors. Such an intellectual shift is particularly difficult in a climate of debate where even to admit consideration of that prospect is viewed as unacceptable, almost treacherous' (Kerley and Wynn, 1990, pp. 8 & 29).

Numerous breaches of the 1988 Act in respect of anti-competitive behaviour have been alleged. The Department of the Environment was said to have received hundreds of malpractice allegations, and at one time to be investigating complaints concerning some 150 authorities (*The Economist*, 9 September 1989, p. 35). Some authorities had decided to modify their practice after informal approaches by the Department of the Environment, and in a few cases formal notices have been served on councils.[1] As an example, a 'Section 13 notice' was served on Bristol City Council which had offered refuse collection, street cleaning and building cleaning as one contract valued at almost £7 million, for which no firms tendered. Although some action has been taken, there is concern that many authorities are being allowed to get away with unfair practices (PSR, no. 16, p. 2; no. 17, pp. 1-2). Among the anti-competitive practices of which some councils have been accused there is that of not awarding a contract, without adequate reason, to a DSO or other contractor whose bid was the lowest.[2] According to one source, consultants exist in respect of ground maintenance to advise local authorities how to prevent a company from winning a contract (CH/B, 1992, p. 8).

Cross-Border Tendering

It is not only private contractors which some councils wish to keep at bay, but also other authorities' DSOs. Cross-border tendering is

---

1 By December 1991, 25 councils had received notices under the 1980 Act (most for apparently failing to achieve the prescribed financial objective, but in three cases the authority appeared to have acted in an anti-competitive manner), and directions had been served on eight of them under the same Act. At the same time, notices had been issued under Section 13 of the 1988 Act to 43 councils; of these, 18 appeared to have failed to achieve the prescribed financial objective, 24 appeared to have acted in an anti-competitive manner, and one appeared to have failed to comply with the detailed specification for the work. Directions had been served under Section 14 of the same Act on 17 of these councils, 11 of which appeared to have acted in an anti-competitive manner (Department of the Environment, December 1991). Directions given under Section 14 have frequently required that the directed authority carry out a re-tendering exercise for the work in question (CQ, p. 12). Tom McGuirk provides a list of authorities and services in respect of which 'Section 13' and 'Section 14' notices have been issued (McGuirk, Appendix A), as does the *Contracts Handbook* which includes also '19a' and '19b' notices under the 1980 Act (CH/B, 1992, Appendix A).

2 For example, Knowsley council's award of a contract for refuse collection to its DSO rather than to a private contractor whose tender was £353,000 less. Knowsley took into account various factors which they claimed more than offset the savings from contracting out: redundancy pay, pension enhancements, accrued holiday pay, wind-up costs of the DLO, and additional supervision costs (RC, p. 39).

regarded as undesirable by many,[1] although opinions on it cross political divides in unexpected ways. The Audit Commission in its reports has quoted evidence of much variation in the efficiency of DSOs, and it is therefore reasonable to suppose that some authorities might obtain better services at lower cost by seeking bids from neighbouring authorities' DSOs; but the Commission has also warned councils that they do not have a general power to trade. A conference hostile to 'privatisation' produced the comment that undertaking work for other authorities allows individual DLOs to concentrate on their strengths and benefit from the expertise of other DLOs (PCR, p. 33). A little cross-border tendering does take place, mainly for ground maintenance.

As the then Junior Environment Minister, David Heathcoat-Amory emphasised, councils have no general power to trade for profit: 'Neither the 1970 Goods and Services Act, nor the 1988 Local Government Act provides a general warrant for DSOs to undertake work for other authorities on a free-for-all basis' (LGIU, 1990, p. 6). However, councils 'may allow the services of staff already engaged for other legitimate purposes who may not be fully employed to be provided by agreement to other public bodies'. Bryan Gould, speaking for the Labour Party, has indicated that his party would not encourage cross-boundary tendering. 'Councils shouldn't compete with each other for work', he said (LGIU, 1990, p. 7). Government policy appears to be inconsistent; Howard Davies has pointed out that in the NHS authorities are actively encouraged to bid for outside work (Burton, 1991, p. 24).

Even co-operation between councils can be difficult to achieve. Brian Whitworth of the Royal Institute of Public Administration has related an experience which came in his first year in local government when he suggested to a local authority that it co-operate with a neighbouring one in the matter of refuse pulverisation. To his consternation he received a letter saying:

'Sir, My committee instructs me to tell you that the refuse of this authority will always be pulverised on machines entirely owned and operated exclusively by this authority' (Whitworth, 1984, p. 46).

---

[1] Guidelines, drawn up by the Association of Metropolitan Authorities with other bodies, restrict 'predatory bids' by local authorities and health authorities. They stipulate that tendering outside an authority's boundaries shall only be undertaken subject to the agreement of both the trade unions in the tendering authority and, where applicable, those in the authority seeking tenders but already providing the service in-house or proposing to do so (CBT). These guidelines have been endorsed by the Labour Party (CCT, pp. 4 & 9-10). Government proposals on CCT for housing management include the sentence: 'It is not proposed that authorities should be enabled to bid for other authorities' contracts' (CQH, p. 18).

Non-Commercial Conditions

Part II of the 1988 Act provides that most non-commercial matters may not be taken into account in awarding contracts, and this particular requirement applies not only to contracts for supply of those services which fall within the defined activities covered by Part I of the Act but also to all contracts for supply of services, goods or materials and for the execution of works.

A survey by the Association of Metropolitan Authorities in England in 1986 found 72 authorities which had policies of stipulating non-commercial conditions in the construction industry, and 53 authorities which had such policies within the purchase and supply of goods and services; 19 authorities even had special units for the purpose.[1] Councils can want a variety of things from these policies: to promote equal opportunities, to ensure fair competition and decent employment standards, to act against companies with connections in particular parts of the world, or to increase the chances of work being retained in-house under CCT (CCS, p. 12). Most authorities used to ask companies to recognise 'appropriate' trade unions, and many made it their business to police suppliers' and contractors' behaviour with regard to the Disabled Persons Act 1945, the Health and Safety Act 1974, the Sex Discrimination Act 1975 and the Race Relations Act 1976. Some concerned themselves with employees' pay or with a company's connections with South Africa or the arms industry (CC, 1986, p. 1). Although it appears that most non-commercial matters may not now be taken into account when inviting contractors to tender, or when choosing the winner, there still seem to be some areas of uncertainty.[2]

The Attitudes of Contractors

The Audit Commission has identified several reasons why private contractors might be reluctant to bid for local authority work in a number of situations (AC87, p. 4):

---

1 In this connection, an unfortunate practice has arisen of using the expression 'contract compliance' in a totally misleading sense which differs considerably from its natural and obvious meaning. According to one publication, the expression 'refers to an authority laying down conditions with which contractors must comply' (Painter, 1990, p. 30), while another states that 'The primary aim of contract compliance is to use the purchasing power of an authority to pursue the policies of the authority' (CCS, p. 12). A third source refers to 'the use of the public sector purchasing power as an instrument of social policy' (CC, p. 1). This perverse use of the expression is illustrated by the statement that 'Contract compliance is outlawed by the Bill ...' (Flynn and Walsh, 1988, p. 12), although it is more natural for compliance with a contract to be required rather than forbidden.

2 A legal opinion obtained by the Inner London Education Authority indicates that the exclusion of 'non-commercial' matters does not affect as many areas as would appear likely at first sight (Kunz, Jones and Spencer, 1989, pp. 9 & 20).

o The emphasis is likely to be on cost, not value; so the opportunity to add extra value and to earn higher margins will be limited. As a result, profit margins are likely to be tight.

o There is no opportunity to build a pre-emptive local position; the contractor will always be vulnerable, since the contract will be regularly subject to competition and in most of the services concerned, entry barriers for competitors are low.

o Any performance shortfall will attract immediate unfavourable publicity locally, and possibly nationally as well. This could easily have knock-on effects elsewhere within the contractor's business. It is for this reason, for instance, that a number of leading companies have declined to bid for NHS catering contracts.

o The potential supplier may not have the local management or capital equipment in place to meet the authorities' requirements.

Another reason why contractors are disinclined to go to the trouble of making bids is that they fear many local authorities are antagonistic towards them, and that the expense of making bids is likely to be wasted. They fear that these authorities will discriminate against them and in favour of their DSOs, that even if they do get the work it will be awarded reluctantly, and that the working relationship will be a difficult one, likely to abound in problems and uncertainties. There seems to be much justification for these fears.[1]

---

[1] Among the complaints of contractors about the way in which they can find themselves treated by councils is that illustrated in a talk by Mike Blundy. This is that contracts are often not awarded to the private contractor despite putting in lower bids:

'Between June 1989 and October 1989 we put in 21 tenders. The results were quite astounding. Two of our bids that we put in were 10 and 20 per cent cheaper than the award price and six were up to 10 per cent below.'

Between October and November 1989 they put in another seven bids to test the market-place again:

'We wanted to find out exactly how much the goal posts had moved—because it is our theory at the moment that prices are being adjusted by DLOs simply to keep the private sector out. At the moment we are of the opinion that this is definitely happening because of those seven bids, three were not awarded to us although we were roughly 10 per cent lower than the awarded price.'

He concluded:

'Finally, an independent person must receive and open the tenders. The private sector is beginning to get evidence that DSO tenders may be altered at tender-opening times. That is a bad thing to have to say to you but the evidence is there' (TT, 1990, p. 57).

Michael Ivens claims that

'The reason why companies do not get the jobs is very often because of corrupt

[Cont'd. on p. 61]

Service Specifications

One important aspect of competitive tendering is the decision which clients must make on the quantity and quality of the services they are to provide, and the details of the specification for the contract. One result of CCT has been to bring about the realisation that hitherto many councils had no specifications for the services they provided, and moreover that the members of many councils were unaware of that fact. One provision of the legislation is that the detailed specification used as the basis for inviting tenders must be adhered to by the DSO as much as by any other successful bidder.[1]

Keith Hartley has defined efficiency as embracing two aspects:

'(i) it is concerned with the lowest-cost method of supplying a *given* quantity and quality of service; and

(ii) it is also concerned with the lowest-cost method of supplying *different* levels of service (i.e. both quality and quantity).' (Hartley, 1984)

The importance of this is that the existing level of service (or any other that is determined without regard to relative costs) might not be the best choice. For example, he points out, a lower level of service might be so much cheaper that the extra cost of the existing provision would be deemed not to be worthwhile. Accordingly he proposes that contractors be invited to bid for alternative levels of service, as well as for a specified level of service (Hartley, 1984, pp. 10 & 14). This useful idea does not appear to have been adopted by many councils. In a survey in 1984/85, out of 75 local authority contracts, only four invited firms to offer alternative specifications for the work (Hartley, 1985, p. 25).

In the first round of tendering under the 1988 Act, Joe Painter found that information was available for only about a fifth of

---

and unfair tendering practices; tendering documents that weigh 5-10 lbs and are designed to put off any prospective tenderer; companies asked to quote for every school or hospital in the area at the same time; . . . loading the tenders with unreal redundancy costs; giving the direct labour department sight of companies' tenders so that they can quote lower (the losses becoming apparent only later)' (Ivens, p. 9).

He gives as an example the case of a health authority which produced nine documents for domestic services, each 18 inches thick. He adds that some District Auditors have been swamped by the weight of illicit practices (Ivens, pp. 9 & 11).

[1] The legal implication of this, as pointed out by solicitors Fox Williams, is that if an authority commits any breach of the specification at all then logically it ceases to have the power to carry out the work. However, they add: 'It is questionable whether an occasional breach of the specification would then have the effect of revoking the Authority's power to carry out the work thereafter or whether the Authority would simply not have the power to carry out the work which it failed to carry out in accordance with its specification' (CCTLGA, 1991, p. 11).

councils' services in respect of the extent of 'cuts', that is, reductions in staffing or wages, or a deterioration in conditions of employment or levels of service. A high proportion were found to involve 'cuts', although Painter rightly points out that the sample was probably unrepresentative (Painter, 1990, pp. 9-10). However, in common with other critics of competition, Painter implies without discussion that 'cuts' are necessarily undesirable. In respect of service levels, this is an unwarranted assumption. In a Utopian world service levels would presumably be not merely maintained but maximised. In the real world there are opportunity costs; more resources spent in one way require less to be spent in other ways. Therefore service levels which happened to be provided—often without any consideration of alternative levels and their corresponding costs—are not necessarily the best for all time. The appropriate level for each service is liable to change, as circumstances change. One of the virtues of competitive tendering has been to focus some attention on service specifications which had previously been taken for granted. Moreover, the tendency of monopoly suppliers to 'overproduce' suggests the possibility that their outputs were too high (although it is their inputs which are more likely to be excessive).

One problem which can arise with contracting out is lack of flexibility in dealing with changing circumstances during the period of a contract. Council members and officers sometimes fear that they will lose control if a service is not provided in-house. Mike Blundy, a director of a leading contractor, replies:

'It's quite simple, providing the contract documents allow you as the client to make alterations at any time during the contract period. So really what I'm saying is you've got to make sure the conditions actually set down that you can make these changes as and when you want. Of course, those changes when you bring them in may mean additional costs. They may mean savings as well' (CP, pp. 31-32).

Mike Queen, director of another business, claims:

'In fact I believe, due to the fact that we are independent contractors, we can act more quickly than the Council themselves to get things done because they have got to put so many things through committees and if they ask us to do it we can get it done' (CP, p. 55).

Much must depend on the council's relationship with its contractors. David Cook, Assistant Director of Education in Lincolnshire, comments in respect of a contract covering 300 establishments:

'The company's greatest strength is their speed in responding to potential difficulties. On a number of occasions their prompt action has enabled solutions to be found in a faster and more effective way than the Council could ever have achieved with the DLO' (SITH, p. 11).

Cecil Rix observes that there are two types of specification: technical and performance. Performance specifications have great advantages over technical specifications, since if the supplier is told exactly how to do something, there is no room for innovation. In any event, a specification must convey unambiguously what one wants other persons to do (Rix, 1984, pp. 33 & 35).

Voluntary Organisations

It is not only businesses which are allowed, or might wish, to bid for local authority work, yet the scope for participation by voluntary organisations is often neglected in discussions of government services.[1] Voluntary organisations are not excluded from submitting bids, although the extent to which they have done so appears to be small or very small. There are many possible complications, such as the tax advantages which charities enjoy, although in most cases a charity would probably have to set up a separate trading company (Kunz, 1989, p. 14). However, there appears to be an increasing trend for contracts to be entered into, although mainly not in the areas covered by CCT, and not necessarily as a result of competitive tendering.[2] Unlike most grants, many contracts and service agreements are made for three years or longer, and this can be an attraction to voluntary groups because of the longer security and ability to plan ahead (CFC, 1990).

---

[1] Voluntary and non-profit organisations are important in the United States, especially in recreation, parks, health services and what are described as 'human services', and the great majority of firefighters are volunteers (Fixler, 1986, pp. 12 & 15). In Holland most social services are provided by large, national voluntary organisations. In the UK, a charity has competed for and won a contract to take over the management of a council-owned residential home. The Women's Royal Voluntary Service has been delivering 'meals on wheels' in many counties for decades. Age Concern has a contracts unit to advise its local groups in contract negotiations (Gutch, 1989, p. 43). Another small example is provided by the National Council for Voluntary Organisations (NCVO), with regard to local voluntary groups which are contracting with the London Borough of Sutton to 'adopt' recycling banks. Under the scheme groups look after and publicise sites in exchange for a fee dependent on the quantity of material collected. The groups contribute their local expertise and thus complement the work of the council's own labour force, which empties the banks and deals with other 'heavy' work (NCVO, p. 8).

[2] For example, some local authorities (and health authorities) draw up contracts with the groups they fund rather than give them grants. Service agreements are another form of aid, mid-way between grants and contracts. They involve considerably more detail than for grants about the commitments made on both sides, while not requiring the use of lawyers as with formal contracts.

It is suggested by Christian Kunz, Rowan Jones and Ken Spencer that an advantage of contracting out to voluntary organisations

'is that it can help to increase the amount of control by the community over public services. Some people feel inadequately represented by the work of their local authority and seem to have little means of influencing even the services which directly affect them' (Kunz *et al.*, 1989, p. 16).

On the other hand, some voluntary organisations 'have established links with the community which make them sensitive to the needs of the population and which enable members of the public to become directly involved'. Running contracted-out services would also allow voluntary organisations 'to prove the traditional voluntary sector claims to greater flexibility, less bureaucracy and more innovation'. Another advantage is that this route 'can lead to a more needs-related provision of public services by eventually breaking down the sometimes rigid compartmentalisation of local authority services'.

With a gradual reduction in the role of local authorities to that of monitoring and regulating, voluntary organisations might secure contracts, for example, for the running of community centres. Another possibility is for a voluntary organisation to be a sub-contractor to a private service provider, for example in welfare catering, environmental work, and sport and leisure management (Kunz *et al.*, 1989, pp. 16-17 & 27). Voluntary organisations are warned, however, to tread very carefully because of the many political disadvantages to bidding:

'A sensitive approach and good timing are absolutely crucial even in preliminary contacts, especially as local authorities continue to be major funders of voluntary organisations' (Kunz *et al.*, 1989, p. 17).

A major consideration for many voluntary organisations is the size of contracts—a subject which is dealt with below (pp. 94 *et seq.*).

Widening Competition

Out of total local government current expenditure of £37,900 million in 1987/88, that on defined activities initially covered by the 1988 Act, according to estimates by the DOE and the Audit Commission, was as shown in Table 2.

Thus the initial effect of the 1988 Act was to subject about 8 per cent of local authority current expenditure to competitive tendering. Other aspects of the work of local authorities for which competitive tendering has been suggested or practised include architectural services, legal services, careers advice, accountancy, personnel, residential care, 'home helps', computing and data processing, school transport, security, printing, fire brigades, police, civic

Table 2:
Local Government Expenditure on Services Covered by the 1988 Act, 1987-88

	£ million
England and Wales	
Refuse collection	450
Street cleaning	200
Catering	600
Building cleaning	300-350
Ground maintenance	450
Vehicle maintenance	300-350
Leisure services	350
Scotland	300
Total	3,000-3,100

Source: CBI2 (1988), p. 19.

amenity sites, pest control, dredging, and the operation of quarries and asphalt plants. Indeed, it has been suggested that in due course the powers within the Act should be used to extend competitive tendering to every local government service (CP, p. 3). This does not imply contracting out of all services; it means testing the efficiency of them all through competition. Few authorities are likely to go as far as Murato, a town in the United States with a population of 40,000, which contracted out 60 separate services (Zetter, 1984, p. 56). That there is scope for improving efficiency in some authorities for a variety of services is indicated by the large variations in the costs of running some council services. For example, employee costs per cremation varied in 1986-87 from £8 to over £80 (AC89b, p. 6).

Professional Services

The Government's intention of widening the scope of CCT to cover professional services was outlined in a consultation document, *The Structure of Local Government in England*. A study was carried out in summer 1991, and the Government's subsequent proposals are outlined below (PCLG, p. 9). The Department of the Environment declined to publish the report prepared in 1991 by PA Consulting Group; but a copy was 'leaked' and a brief account has been pub-

Table 3:
**Numbers of Staff Engaged in Professional Services
in Local Government, 1991**

Corporate services	
Corporate and administrative services	49,000
Finance	67,300
Personnel	11,100
Legal	7,850
Computing	14,250
Construction services	
Architecture	18,700
Engineering	50,250
Property management	14,600
Regulatory services	
Planning	26,650
Consumer protection	4,700
Environmental health	17,100
Direct public services	
Libraries (short-term)	34,550
Libraries (long-term)	34,550

Source: Burton (1992a), p. 10.

lished. According to this, the report concludes that for construction services and most direct public services competitive tendering is straightforward, that for corporate activities it is more difficult but still feasible, and that most regulatory services are poor candidates, with problems outweighing the benefits. The report recommends that, where appropriate, a defined proportion of each service area—varying from 15 per cent to 80 per cent—be subject to CCT.

The estimated numbers of staff in Britain for these sectors are set out in Table 3. The estimated cost in all four sectors is £6,300 million a year. However, the staffing costs of services suitable for tendering are put at around £2,600 million. The report recommends the introduction of trading accounts for all affected services, and approval for local authorities to trade with each other (Burton, 1992a).

The consultants considered that extending competition in these areas is likely to cause 'a more profound change than any other local government legislation since 1974', and they reported that most managers were opposed to such an extension of CCT. The reaction of authorities to the Government's proposals was gauged by *Local Government Chronicle* which asked the chief executives of 523 authorities in Britain for their opinions (Keenan, 1991). The result was that as many as 81 per cent of the 283 chief executives replying did not think the costs of contracting out central services—administration, legal, finance, personnel, and information technology—would be offset by savings.[1]

Nevertheless, some authorities are already using the private sector selectively, buying in services for reasons of efficiency or pressure of work in specific areas: security and printing, debt collection, software development and maintenance, litigation and special legal projects, and personnel advertising and payroll work. Nearly 10 per cent (approximately £19 million) of total legal costs of local government are bought in (Robertson, 1992, p. 54). However, the idea of tendering for central services is said still to provoke vehement opposition among professionals. A consistent complaint was about the compulsion to tender, with one respondent commenting:

> 'The main danger lies in once again operating within a prescriptive, inhibiting, stultifying framework which will reduce the opportunity for innovation, initiative, flexibility and end progressive management processes' (Keenan, 1991).

How justified these fears are remains to be seen. The five functions covered by the survey are dealt with by only 105,000 centrally employed staff[2]—a very small proportion of the total employed by local authorities.

Professional services cannot be assessed as easily as can many other services, so that competitive tendering requires to be approached with thought and care. Michael Wigginton has observed, in

---

[1] The proportion varied somewhat in relation to party-political control, those respondents thinking that savings would not offset costs being 71 per cent in the case of Conservative-controlled authorities, 76 per cent for Labour-controlled authorities, and more for authorities controlled by other parties or by none. One reason for the doubts was that 70 per cent expected that, if these services were contracted out, they would require more monitoring than contracted out technical services.

[2] Some 73 per cent of the chief executives expect that competitive pressures will lead to a reduction in this number. According to Paul Keenan, the clearest area of growth for the private sector lies in information technology where it already has a role in 39 per cent of authorities; on the other hand, 12 per cent of chief executives did not think that private-sector involvement was appropriate even in this area (Keenan, 1991).

the context of architecture, that 'the method by which briefs [specifications] are set to the competitors, and the criteria by which the winner is selected, will be critical' (Wigginton, 1991, p. 9). The possible need for different procedures is, fortunately, acknowledged in a government White Paper (CQBB, 1991, p. 24).

Fire Brigades

Local authorities were given a statutory duty to maintain fire brigades in 1938, a responsibility which was removed from them in 1941 on the formation of a national fire service, and in 1947 given to a smaller number of councils than before the War. The fire service in the UK costs over £800 million and employs some 39,000 whole-time firemen, 17,000 part-time firemen, and 8,000 control-room and non-uniformed employees. By contrast, West Germany's voluntary brigades, for example, had over 900,000 members. While the UK's fire brigades are generally considered to be very good in terms of the service provided, they appear to offer poor value for money.

The cost of fire protection in the UK in 1984, as a proportion of gross domestic product, was two and a half times that in Denmark, where the service is largely contracted out. In his study of this subject, Michael Simmonds points out that the Fire Services Act of 1947 already allows a fire authority to make arrangements with any other fire authority or other persons for the discharge of any or all of its functions. In view of the success of fire services contracted out in Denmark and the United States, there is a strong case for testing and improving, through competitive tendering, the efficiency of fire services in the UK (Simmonds, 1989, pp. 3, 5, 7 & 41). A study by the Audit Commission found the fire service in the UK to be 35 per cent more expensive than that in the Netherlands, although very similar in the standards observed. Among the various reasons suggested are our rigid employment conditions which prevent sensible use being made of the most highly qualified employees (AC86, sections 30-37).

Police

Many aspects of police work could be contracted out, with the advantage that trained policemen would be able to give more time to those functions which would most benefit from their expertise.[1]

---

[1] Services suggested for contracting out include registration procedures associated with aliens, escorting of abnormal loads, surveillance of motorway traffic, provision of security at courts, the service and execution of process, police driver training, communications training, physical training, photography and printing. The

[Cont'd. on p. 69]

Contracting out of the whole of a police force's functions would probably be too radical a step for any British government to contemplate. However, there is a history of private provision in Britain before the introduction of borough and county police forces around the middle of the last century, and there is limited but interesting experience in recent years of private services abroad (Gage, 1982; Evans, 1991, pp. 18, 22-23 & 38).

Police expenditure by central and local government has risen by an average of 12½ per cent a year for over a decade, but the level of crime has risen rapidly and 65 per cent of reported crimes are unsolved. The police services are not immune to the forces of inefficiency, as the Audit Commission has pointed out. Few police forces have specified the standards of service they intend to meet, and fewer still monitor their actual performance. For example, most forces do not know how long their telephone operators take to answer calls from the public, or the delay before their patrol officers arrive at incidents. Costs of transport are unnecessarily high, as a result of poor management of vehicle fleets.[1]

Government Proposals

As expressed by the Financial Secretary to the Treasury, Francis Maude, the Government's attitude to contracting out is as follows:

'We have no ideological preference either for buying in services from the private sector or supplying them within the public sector. But we *do* have an ideological preference for *competition*, as the key method for ensuring best value for taxpayers' money, and best quality for the customer' (Maude, 1992, p. 1).

In November 1991 the Government published both a consultation paper, *Competing for Quality*, and a Treasury White Paper, *Competing for Quality—Buying Better Public Services*, and in March of the following year the Local Government Act 1992 incorporated some, but not all, of the proposals in the consultation

---

Metropolitan Police have contracted out wheel-clamping and removal of vehicles. The Home Office have identified photography, fingerprint examination, road safety, vehicle examination, driving instruction, physical training, personnel administration and patrol-room duties as areas where civilians could be employed rather than uniformed officers.

[1] Howard Davies, when Controller of the Audit Commission, stated that:

'An awful lot of measurement of police effectiveness could be done and the police have been somewhat coy about measuring their performance in the past. They should open themselves up more and be prepared to discuss actual figures and performance measures. Their only chance of turning round the adverse trend in public confidence is to take the public into their confidence' (Evans, 1991, pp. 13-20).

paper. The Act's effect is not automatic since it depends on government action in the form of Orders laid before Parliament to bring its provisions into operation.[1] The declared intention is to clarify, strengthen and improve the law requiring competition in the supply of various local services. The consultation paper states that

'too many authorities have sought to bend the rules laid down by the legislation, to cushion their workforces against the full force of competition—and thus to deny their own charge-payers the financial and performance benefits that competition can deliver' (CQ, 1991, p. 4).

In addition to the new legislation, the Government proposed to make further use of their existing powers under Part III of the 1980 Act and Part I of the 1988 Act.

Regulations proposed under existing legislation would require those in an authority who prepare the DSO tender not to be involved in the selection of potential suppliers or in the subsequent evaluation of tenders. They should also not receive, from the client side of the organisation, information about the preparation of a tender which is not available to external tenderers. Exceptions might be made for smaller authorities and for units within them, such as schools, which could face difficulties with these regulations. There are five main stages in the contracting process, and it is proposed to specify a minimum period of time for each stage, in line with advice already given to authorities (CQ, pp. 6-7).

It is proposed to amend the 1980 and 1988 Acts to provide a power to make regulations which would specify the cost items authorities may, or may not, take into account when comparing tenders. It is proposed also to use regulations to ensure that actual costs or savings incurred, if an external tender is accepted, are compared with those incurred if an in-house bid is accepted.[2]

The number of local authority employees engaged on the professional and technical activities considered in the consultation paper is between about 250,000 and 300,000, and the annual cost of their work is estimated to be between £5,000 million and £6,000 million. Extension of compulsory competitive tendering to

---

[1] Draft regulations, on tender evaluation and timing of stages in the tendering process, were issued for consultation in June 1992 (*Municipal Journal*, 19 June 1992, p. 5; 3 July 1992, pp. 18-19).

[2] This would be done by calculating the allowable costs and savings of each option at constant prices, and discounting them at a recommended real discount rate (currently 6 per cent). Local authorities would be required to assume that any annual savings from contracting-out would continue for 10 years, and this treatment would apply, for example, to redundancy costs and to savings from the sale of assets not wanted by an external contractor. A further proposal is that the cost of a performance bond be subtracted from an external bid (CQ, pp. 8-9).

much of this work is proposed. The activities concerned are in three major groups:[1]

- o direct public services: the management of theatres and arts facilities, library support services, parking services;

- o construction-related services: architecture, engineering, property management;

- o corporate services: corporate and administrative, legal, financial, personnel, computing.

There is already extensive use made by some authorities of outside architectural, engineering and legal services. Some professional and technical services, however, would not be suitable for CCT.

The Government proposes to require each local authority to establish and maintain internal trading accounts for all corporate professional services, whether subject to competition or not. As an alternative to requiring specified elements of these services to be exposed to competition, it is tentatively proposed to require that a proportion of the total value of work in each service be so exposed, thus allowing authorities considerable flexibility in implementing the requirement. These proportions would vary according to service, possibly from 15 per cent for corporate and administrative work to 80 per cent for computing work (CQ, 1991, pp. 17-33).

Extension of CCT to several manual activities not previously covered is another proposal, although exceptions might still be made for some aspects of the work (CQ, pp. 14-16). These activities are: cleaning of police buildings; maintenance of police vehicles; maintenance of fire-service vehicles; provision of home-to-school transport where centrally organised. The extension of CCT to Northern Ireland, starting with refuse collection on 1 January 1994, was prepared for by draft regulations issued in the middle of 1992 (*Municipal Journal*, 10 July 1992, p. 9).

Housing management was covered by separate proposals made in June 1992, whereby tendering for the management of council homes would be required. In England and Wales councils manage

---

[1] Extension of CCT to the management of theatre and arts facilities would involve the financial objective that income meet expenditure. The income would be allowed to include any subsidy made available by the authority, on condition that the subsidy is made available to all tenderers, and that the amount of subsidy is in the contract specification. The inclusion of parking services in the list refers only to the provision and management of such services under the Road Traffic Act 1991 (which is effective initially only in London).

some 4 million properties, worth some £130,000 million at vacant-possession value. This is about a fifth of the total housing stock. The number of non-manual staff employed in housing by local authorities is over 55,500, having increased over the past decade by more than 50 per cent. The standard of council housing management varies considerably, as do costs. Uncollected rents amount to hundreds of millions of pounds, and the proportion of authorities' properties held empty varies in England from 0·1 to 9·7 per cent. Clearly some authorities are much less efficient than others.

The Government proposed to extend CCT to include housing management, but first to invite some authorities to conduct experimental tendering exercises. The market is likely to offer limited competition in the early stages, and the introduction of CCT would be phased over several years. Although authorities' own staff might win many of the initial contracts, tenants were expected to benefit from the targets and performance measures imposed by the contracts. Authorities would be allowed to decide the size, shape and scope of contracts, so long as they were not anti-competitive (CQH, 1992, pp. 2, 8 & 16-17).

FOUR

The Results of Competitive Tendering

This chapter examines the extent of competition for the provision of government services, the extent to which tendering resulted in contracting out, and the savings which competition produced. Consideration is then given to employees' losses and gains, costs incurred by councils as clients, the discovery by councils of the consumer, the quality of services and the need to monitor them, and the incidence of contract failure. Finally we look at the size and length of contracts, the effect of contract size on competition, the effect of competition on local authority management and on direct service organisations, and management buy-outs.

The Extent of Competition

According to one assessment, the Local Government Act 1988 requires that nearly 2,000 local government service contracts, with a total value of £2,700 million, be subjected (progressively over a period of years) to compulsory competitive tendering (*The Economist*, 9 September 1989, p. 35). The number of manual workers employed on work subject to CCT under the 1980 and 1988 Acts is thought to be at least 250,000, and the total value of the work is estimated as in the region of £5,000 million (CQ, 1991, p. 14). There have been various studies of the effects of the 1988 Act, but far fewer studies of the effects of the 1980 Act which was much less extensive in its CCT requirements.

In the Centre for Local Economic Strategies' report (1990), out of 326 services awarded to a DSO in the first round of CCT, information was obtained on the degree of competition in 102 cases. These might, however, not be representative since the degree of reporting could be related to the extent of competition. Of the 326 cases of in-house success, competition was reported for 22 per cent, no competition for at least 9 per cent, and there was no information for 69 per cent. Adding services which were contracted out, and assuming that there was competition (at least from a DSO) in all such cases, produces the following results: competition in 42

Table 4:
**Survey of Contractors Applying for Work
in Various Services of Local Government, 1992**

	(A)	(B)	(C)	(D)	(E)
		Average Number			%
Building cleaning	19·0	12·5	8·3	4·6	19
Refuse collection, of which	13·0	11·1	6·1	3·2	9
Refuse collection and other cleaning combined	12·8	10·3	5·3	2·8	. . .
Other cleaning	10·7	8·3	6·1	3·2	13
Vehicle maintenance	11·6	8·5	6·2	3·1	25
Catering (education and welfare)	6·3	4·3	3·5	1·4	61
Catering (other)	9·2	6·7	5·7	2·3	36
Ground maintenance	12·3	9·8	7·0	4·0	14
Sports and leisure management	6·5	4·6	3·9	1·7	. . .
Overall	11·1	8·2	5·8	3·0	. . .

. . . = not available or not applicable.

Source: CCTIS (1991), pp. 2, 6, 12, 19, 24-26, 31-32, 37, 41-42 & 49.

per cent of cases, no competition in 7 per cent, and no information available for 51 per cent (Painter, 1990, pp. 14-15). In the *Local Government Chronicle* survey of July 1990, there was no external bid in two out of every five contracts offered by Labour councils, and in one in six offered by Conservative councils (LGC90, p. 12).

In the Local Government Management Board survey of April 1992, covering 3,475 contracts in England and Wales, the proportion of contracts won without competition varied from 61 per cent for catering (education and welfare) to 9 per cent for refuse collection. Table 4 shows the average numbers of contractors (A) applying for work in each activity, (B) completing the questionnaire, (C) invited to tender, and (D) submitting a tender. Column (E) shows the proportion of contracts won without competition (figures given here are rounded to the nearest whole number). Competition has generally been less in the North of England than in the South. However, for refuse collection and catering (education and welfare) there has been little regional variation.

There has been a shortage of private contractors able and willing both to take on the sort of work required by local authorities and to undertake contracts of the size envisaged. The *Municipal Journal* made the comment in November 1990 that,

'Although our survey has recorded approximately 95 separate contractors, plus additional small local firms, a staggering 45 per cent of all the authorities questioned claimed to have had insufficient response from other interested parties.' (Pollard, 1990, p. 22)

Of the remainder, 40 per cent were satisfied with the response, and 15 per cent expressed no opinion. Mark Pollard suggests several possible reasons for this: a lack of suitably qualified contractors; the large size of many of the contracts, especially for refuse collection and catering; and the size of the performance bonds required of contractors. On the last point, it is suggested that this could also explain the late withdrawal of some firms who, having won one contract, cannot afford to compete for another as their credit worthiness is soon used up by these bonds (Pollard, 1990).

A survey of the first three rounds or phases of CCT in Scotland, produced by the Convention of Scottish Local Authorities (COSLA), covers 62 of Scotland's 65 local authorities for the first two phases, and 54 for the third phase. The survey covers a total of 286 individual contracts, subject to CCT under the 1988 Act.[1] Of the 286 individual contracts, no contractors (excluding the in-house DSO) at all applied to tender for 12 per cent, while for nearly 15 per cent only one applied; the proportion for which three or more contractors applied was 67 per cent, and the proportion for which at least three contractors were invited to bid was 63 per cent. However, for 51 per cent of contracts no contractor submitted a bid, and the proportion for which three or more competing bids were received was only 16 per cent. In the third phase, out of 95 invitations to tender, for 89 per cent no bids were received from contractors. In total, over the three phases 1,064 invitations to tender were issued to 199 potential tenderers, and 283 bids were received from 101 tenderers. Of these individual tenderers, 27 (17 private contractors and 10 other DSOs) were successful, winning between them 34 contracts (CCT2, 1991).

---

[1] These were sometimes combined, so that there were 170 contract packages, 140 of which were for single contracts but 30 for two or more contracts; 18 contract packages (accounting for 146 contracts) had two or more different activities in combination. There were 67 contract packages for activities with a value of less than £100,000 a year, eight of which were put out to tender, while for the remaining 59 exemption was claimed under the *de minimis* rule. The average length of contracts was 4·4 years.

Clearly there has been a considerable lack of competitors, with the result that in some areas of the country competitive tendering has been more nominal than real. It could be that this is partly due to union-led opposition to CCT and contracting out—opposition which has been particularly strong in some areas, and particularly effective where there are close links between trade unions and the majority party in the local council.

The Extent of Contracting Out

The first round of contracts under the 1988 Act started on 1 August 1989. The results of surveys by several trade unions and by *Municipal Journal* were collated and analysed by Joe Painter and published in August 1990 (Painter, 1990). Information was available on 362 (70 per cent) of the 514 councils in Britain, but of these 63 were exempt from CCT under the *de minimis* rules, so that the combined survey covered the remaining 299 councils. Between them these authorities put 438 services up for tender in the first round. Of these, 326 or 74·4 per cent were won by the council's DSO or by another council's DSO; 21·5 per cent were won by a private contractor (or by a management buy-out of the council's former DSO), and in 4·1 per cent of cases the service, having been divided into several contracts, was won by a mixture of private and in-house contractors (Painter, 1990, pp. 9-10). In considering these results, one factor must be that DSOs had the advantage of being familiar with the work for which they were tendering.

Varying DSO Success Rate

The proportion of tenders won by DSOs varied considerably, according to both type of service and type of council. The service with the lowest proportion of DSO success was building cleaning (57 per cent), while that with the highest was school and welfare catering (97 per cent). In the latter case, the relatively low profit margins and the large size of many contracts are among factors considered to have been responsible for the limited interest of the private sector. As regards type of authority, the highest rates of in-house wins were found among the metropolitan district and the Scottish district councils. They are also located in areas where the trade union movement is particularly strong, and it is suggested that this may have deterred private contractors (Painter, 1990, p. 11).

The analysis of the first round of CCT shows that the degree of DSO success varied very significantly in relation to the party political orientation of councils. Only a tiny minority of the services covered by the survey were contracted out by Labour councils, whereas partial or complete contracting out by Conservative councils occurred in over half of all services. Councils controlled by other parties or by none, or in which no party had an overall majority, were intermediate in the extent of their contracting out (Painter, 1990, pp. 12-13). Although these differences could be due partly to regional and other variations, it seems very likely that the explanation is, at least in part, that many councils have obstructed contracting out in accordance with party political considerations.

According to a survey covering contracts awarded up to 1 August 1990 and some starting in January 1991, out of a total of 1,772 contracts, 72 per cent had been won by in-house DSOs, 2·8 per cent by other DSOs, 24·3 per cent by private contractors, and 0·8 per cent by management buy-out firms (MBOs). The share won by private contractors varied from over 39 per cent for building cleaning (less than 10 per cent by value) to 19 per cent for vehicle maintenance, and just 1 per cent for education and welfare catering (PSA). A slightly different analysis by SCAT, based on 809 contracts up to the end of February 1990, found that 78 per cent were won by in-house DSOs, 2½ per cent by other DSOs, and 15½ per cent by private contractors, while 3½ per cent were shared by DSOs and private contractors (PAC, 1990, p. 20).

A report by SCAT and Sheffield City Council on refuse collection and street cleaning found that in these areas 220 contracts worth an estimated £250 million were subject to tendering during 1989 and early 1990. Private contractors won 25 per cent of the 110 refuse collection contracts, 18 per cent of the 55 street cleaning contracts, and 11 per cent of the 55 combined contracts. Of the 170 contracts for which the value was known, private contractors won, in the same three categories respectively, 30, 15 and 14·4 per cent by value. Most successes for private contractors were in District Councils (39 out of a total of 44) (RC, pp. 37-38). The report points out that 'there is no doubt that the size and political composition of local authorities' has been a factor of importance in the pattern of tendering across the country (RC, p. 47). The political complexion of a council is, however, perhaps less important than its size. It is the authorities with large in-house workforces in which trade union power is strongest.

The extent of contracting out has fluctuated over the first three rounds of CCT, according to surveys published in *Municipal Journal*. At the close of the first round of tendering in August 1989 the proportion of in-house wins stood at 77 per cent. Over the

Table 5:
Numbers of Contracts Awarded to DSOs (Internal and External), MBOs and Private Contractors, 1988 to 1992*

Activity	DSOs (internal) No.	DSOs (external) No.	MBOs No.	Private No.	Total No.
Building cleaning	446	13	4	269	732
Refuse collection	319	–	9	106	434
Other cleaning	164	5	1	38	208
Grounds maintenance	652	83	12	196	943
Schools and welfare catering	159	–	–	14	173
Other catering	132	2	–	44	178
Vehicle maintenance	188	6	–	48	242
Sports and leisure management	180	1	16	26	223
Total	2,240	110	42	741	3,133

– = Nil.

*Period covered includes contracts awarded before the 1988 Act up to publication of McGuirk (May 1992).

Source: McGuirk (1992), pp. ii, 8, 15, 22, 31, 40-41, 48 & 57-58.

following months this grew to between 79 and 80 per cent, thereafter falling to the figure of 76 per cent reported in November 1990, with 21 per cent being won by the private sector, 2 per cent by cross-boundary tenders, and 1 per cent by management buy-outs (Pollard, 1990).

The Institute of Public Finance maintains records on contracts dating from before 1988; by early 1992 the number of contracts included was some 4,000. The numbers of contracts awarded in total and the numbers won by internal and external DSOs, MBO businesses and private contractors are given in Table 5. Refuse collection also had combined street cleaning functions in 141 cases; two authorities included building cleaning as well; 30 authorities included the maintenance of refuse collection vehicles.

The total annual value of all recorded contracts for each activity, and the percentages of that value won by in-house DSOs, other DSOs, MBO businesses and private contractors, are given in Table 6.

Table 6:
**Annual Value of Recorded Contracts Awarded
by Service, and Shares Obtained by DSOs, MBOs,
and Private Contractors, 1988 to 1992***

	Value of all contracts £m.	In-house DSOs %	Other DSOs %	MBOs %	Private %
Activity					
Building cleaning	366	84·3	0·9	0·6	14·2
Refuse collection	517	74·3	–	3·9	21·8
Other cleaning	132	82·7	0·8	0·3	16·2
Grounds maintenance	315	80·6	3·4	1·1	14·9
Schools and welfare catering	267	96·6	–	–	3·4
Other catering	79	91·6	0·2	–	8·2
Vehicle maintenance	144	79·1	2·3	–	18·6

– = Nil.

*As for Table 5.

Source: McGuirk (1992), pp. 11, 18, 26, 35, 40-41, 44, 52 & 58.

The proportion by value won by private contractors varies from about 3 per cent to nearly 22 per cent, while that won by in-house DSOs ranges from over 74 per cent to nearly 98 per cent. Cross-boundary contracting is most notable in the case of ground maintenance.

In the Local Government Management Board's survey of 3,475 contracts awarded in England and Wales, the in-house DSO success rate varied, in terms of numbers of contracts won, from 58 per cent for building cleaning to 94 per cent for catering (education and welfare). However, by value in-house DSOs were more successful, winning between 75 and 97½ per cent of work according to the category. In 173 authorities DSOs had a 100 per cent success rate, while 26 authorities (24 non-metropolitan districts and two London boroughs) have no recorded DSO contracts. DSO success rates have been highest in metropolitan districts. They also vary geographically: for example, in building cleaning DSOs won every contract in the North West but only 35 per cent (by number) in the East Midlands. In refuse collection DSOs won every contract in Wales but only 52 per cent of those in London (CCTIS, 1991, pp. 7, 12-13, 20 & 37).

Since the introduction of CCT over 400 contracts have been

awarded for street cleaning. According to CD-C Research, one in six of these contracts has been awarded to the private sector (often to French-owned companies). Interestingly, while private contractors have won only one in seven contracts for street cleaning alone, they have gained nearly one in four of those that combine refuse collection with street cleaning. Moreover, their share of such combined contracts rose from 15 per cent in 1989 and 1990 to 35 per cent in 1991 (CH, 1992, pp. 8-9). It seems that the aim of authorities which offered these large combined contracts was to make them unattractive to nearly all private contractors, but that this policy was only temporarily successful.

Of 372 contracts for ground maintenance let between 1989 and 1992, private companies hold 112 contracts (30 per cent). There are 53 private companies operating ground maintenance contracts, many of them extremely small. The most successful company is Brophy plc with 45 contracts. Some authorities are said to encourage small firms by offering contracts such that only local firms would be interested (CH/B, 1992, p. 7).

In a survey of the first three phases of CCT in Scotland, of the total of 286 contracts, in-house DSOs won 88 per cent, other DSOs won 3½ per cent, and private contractors won 8½ per cent. Of the 275 contracts whose values were ascertained, and on the basis of first-year contract values, in-house DSOs won over 97 per cent, other DSOs less than ½ per cent, and private contractors 2½ per cent. Of the 24 contracts won by private contractors, 13 were for ground maintenance, 8 for refuse collection, 2 for building cleaning, and 1 for vehicle maintenance (CCT2, 1991, pp. 3-5).

Before and After CCT

A survey by the *Municipal Year Book* in March 1984 of the 547 authorities in the UK, which produced the very good response rate of 93 per cent, found 190 which had contracted out at least one service (or in some cases part of a service). In many cases contracts were for a short period, often as short as a year. Catering in parks and leisure centres had long made use of private services, and there were many contracts for mowing work. Three years later the number contracting out at least one service was 223, although 21 authorities had abandoned contracting out in the intervening period (*Municipal Year Book*, 1985, p. 448; 1988, p. 397).

A survey in *Local Government Chronicle* in July 1989 indicates the extent of contracting out just before the extension of compulsory competition. The survey was for the financial year 1988/89, and 300 authorities replied—a response rate of 59 per cent. Less than one-third of all authorities replying had put contracts out to tender; less than half the Conservative-controlled councils had done so, and less than a fifth of Labour-controlled councils. Conservative councils awarded 46 contracts (by value 25 per cent) to private contractors (including two to management buy-outs), against 33 in-house (by value 47·3 per cent), 11 mixed and three to other authorities. By contrast, Labour councils awarded two contracts (by value 0·2 per cent) to private contractors, against 13 in-house (by value 99·5 per cent), two mixed and one to another authority. The authors comment that private-sector contractors might well decide that tendering for business in some authorities is a waste of time and effort (LGC89).

The following year's survey, for 1989/90, covered a period in which the extension of CCT had begun to take effect. This time only 231 authorities (45 per cent) replied, but information was gathered on 476 contracts totalling at least £1,597 million. This figure is an underestimate inasmuch as some councils were unwilling to give values for any of their reported contracts. Out of 476 contracts, 374 (by value 82·5 per cent) were awarded in-house, 20 (by value 2·6 per cent) went to other councils, and 82 (by value 14·8 per cent) to the private sector including management buy-outs (LGC90).

Contracting-out of service provision has not been the principal effect of competitive tendering. However, some contracting-out is essential if private contractors are to feel that it is worth competing for council business.

Savings from Competition

The main purpose of competitive tendering is efficiency in the use of public resources. However, several of the organisations which conduct surveys on CCT have not even asked local authorities about the savings they have made, apparently because many authorities are reluctant to provide such information, even when they are able to do so. Where figures are available, increased efficiency has very often been found to result from competitive tendering. Although there is some evidence that savings are greater when the work is contracted out, as a result of competition substantial savings are often obtained whether or not the work is retained in-house.

The INLOGOV Study

In one detailed survey, that by INLOGOV, of the 40 panel authorities asked, only 24 were able to provide useful answers on the financial consequences of competition, and few of those provided all the information required. Another limitation, but an understandable one, is that the figures were for tender prices rather than for outturn costs (Walsh, K., 1991, p. 121). However, the figures do provide comparisons for 129 contracts covering 59 service areas. Adjustments were made, where necessary, to allow for inflation; but no allowance was made for changes (mostly improvements) in the quality of services provided. The overall result was an average estimated annual cost at constant prices 5·7 per cent lower than that before competition. The variation in results was considerable, however, ranging from an increase in estimated cost of 25·9 per cent to a reduction of 48·9 per cent. Changes in estimated costs varied according to the type of service, though the figures are based on fairly small samples so cannot be relied on strongly. Average savings ranged from 1·8 per cent for school and welfare catering to 17·1 per cent for cleaning of buildings, with costs having increased by 5·6 per cent in the case of street cleaning, where the result was due to improvement of standards (Walsh, K., 1991, pp. 125-6).

These figures do not take into account some factors, such as changes in leasing agreements, redundancy payments, and income from sale of equipment. Local authorities were therefore asked to provide overall estimates of all the costs or savings in each defined service, so as to estimate the total continuing annual savings or additional costs resulting from competition. Of 47 cases quoted, costs rose in 12 cases (but in five of these standards had been improved), and fell in 35 cases. The average result was a saving of 7·0 per cent, while the range of results was +14·6 to −49·7 per cent (Walsh, K., 1991, pp. 126-7). Little or no mention is made of any fall in standards, whereas standards were improved in nine of the 47 cases, so in terms of cost for a given standard of service, it appears that the average saving was probably somewhat greater than 7 per cent. The main reason given for altered costs after tendering was changed productivity (quoted 31 times as reducing costs). Other factors included changed pay levels (mentioned 10 times as reducing costs, six times as increasing them) and changed standards (mentioned 17 times as increasing costs, twice as reducing them) (Walsh, K., 1991, p. 128).

Audit Commission Findings

According to Steve Evans, a senior manager with the Audit Commission, initial results of the 1988 Act have confirmed the Commission's expectations that authorities could achieve savings of up to 20 per cent in contract price. These expectations had come in for some criticism for supposedly exaggerating the potential for efficiency improvements. However, the Audit Commission's information from auditors was that one or two authorities were achieving large savings (usually on contracts of smaller value), and that the majority find that they are saving something in the range of 10 to 30 per cent. Interestingly, these savings are being made irrespective of whether the work is won in-house or by private contractors. Moreover, in general these improvements come from improved productivity, not from reductions in wages to workers or conditions of service. The only exception to this general rule may be in building cleaning, where there are some indications that wages may be less than they were before (TT, 1990, pp. 18-19). It is noteworthy that the average savings reported by INLOGOV are markedly lower than those found in a number of other studies such as those of the Audit Commission and that discussed next.

Refuse Collection

A detailed study of refuse collection by the Centre for Business Strategy at the London School of Economics showed that, where services have been tendered and awarded to private contractors, costs are broadly 22 per cent lower once relevant factors, such as quality of service and geographical features, have been taken into account. In cases where services had been put to tender, but where the award had gone to the DSO, costs were 17 per cent lower than when there was no tender; however, the difference between the two figures (22 and 17 per cent) was within the margin of statistical uncertainty. Of the 22 per cent cost reduction on contracts awarded to private contractors, it was found that 17 per cent resulted from higher productivity in the use of labour and vehicles.[1] Of the 17 per cent cost reduction on contracts awarded to DSOs, however, 7 per cent was attributed to higher productivity in the use of labour and vehicles; no explanation was offered for the remaining 10 per cent (TT, 1990, pp. 27-29).

Local Government Chronicle Survey

In the survey of 1988/89 contracts published by *Local Government Chronicle* in July 1989, the overall response was 59 per cent, but of the 300 councils replying many failed to identify the savings they made. The proportion unable or unwilling to reveal their savings varied according to service between 37 and 64 per cent. Over a

---

[1] At least three factors are thought to contribute to the remaining 5 per cent: improved productivity in the use of other inputs, lower wages or less favourable conditions of employment, and better choice of technology (such as better matching of vehicle size to population density).

third (36 per cent) of councils failed or refused to identify savings for every one of their services. The total value of the contracts was £251 million, while the *reported* savings totalled £26 million. In the following year's survey, contract values totalled £1,597 million. Total reported savings were £86·5 million, and total reported costs were £11·9 million; however, no indication was given of the value of the contracts to which these figures relate, or of the 'failure rate' in reporting savings or costs, but it can be inferred that the latter was high (LGC89 & LGC90).

PULSE Assessment

According to *Public Service Review* (No. 17), published by PULSE, annual savings from contracting out services to the private sector (thus excluding savings produced in-house) after the first two rounds of competitive tendering were over £42 million. Over 250 local authorities have contracted out at least one service. However, figures for savings are unavailable in the case of many of the contracts listed by the publication, so that total savings must be appreciably greater.

Scotland

In their survey of the first round of CCT in Scotland, Kerley and Wynn comment warily:

'Though the issue of "savings" through CCT is contentious and unclear, what can be said is that the enforcement of contract-based services, even where DSOs have won contracts with no alternative bids lodged, has of itself forced a reduction of costs and/or an increase in productivity. In the cases of major services, those savings comparing tender prices with projected direct budget costs, have sometimes been very substantial' (Kerley and Wynn, 1991, p. 32).

They point to the need, in any convincing financial evaluation of the effects of CCT, to consider the quality of service provided and the total of real costs incurred in the overall exercise of moving to contract-based services. These matters are considered below.

Highway Maintenance

A study of the effects of the Local Government, Planning and Land Act 1980 in respect of highway maintenance was produced by the Audit Commission in 1991. In 1987 and 1988 regulations made under the Act required more work to be exposed to competition. Previously 70 per cent of work below £50,000 could be awarded to the DLO without competition, whereas after April 1988 only 40 per cent of work below £25,000 could be so awarded. Despite these changes, some DLOs continue to be awarded the majority of their authority's highway maintenance work as of right.[1]

The Audit Commission studied 13 authorities in detail, and sent a questionnaire to 155 authorities. Six of the 13 authorities were ones which had awarded much of the work to their DLOs as of right, and were thus forced by the regulation changes to expose more work to competition, while the other seven (the control group) had always exposed more work than required to competition. This enabled useful comparisons to be made between the two groups. The net effect of the regulation changes was that authorities which were forced to put much more work out to tender made savings of 15 per cent on the work newly exposed to competition compared with the control group. There had been some increases in staff so as to implement the changes, but in many cases the increases were only redressing long-standing weaknesses in supervision. Moreover, the cost of additional staff was far outweighed by the savings.

The wider questionnaire-based survey supported the in-depth research.[2] Both reveal that officers were convinced that there had been non-financial benefits from increased competition. These included clearer managerial responsibilities, better specification of work, and improved planning of work (AC91a, pp. 1-2, 4-7, 14-16 & 19).

Employees' Losses and Gains

The expectation of most employees in local government has been one of total security of employment. This security has been provided at taxpayers' expense, and CCT has had the result of diminishing it. To this extent at least, these employees have suffered a loss. Those who argue that competition is bad because it leads to job losses rarely state that overstaffing is good because it retains jobs, though this seems to be their assumption. However, as the French economist Bastiat pointed out, those who do not break windows 'deprive' glaziers of work, but that does not make window-breaking a useful activity, since—disregarding the transfer of wealth—the community as a whole loses from it.

---

[1] On the other hand, the majority of construction work has always been put out to tender. Annual expenditure by local authorities in England and Wales on their own roads is about £2,400 million. Figures produced by CIPFA for general highway and sewerage work suggest that DLOs do about 43 per cent of the work, and contractors about 57 per cent.

[2] While 11 per cent of respondents said that the quality of work had deteriorated as a result of changes in the regulations, 15 per cent stated that it had improved; the rest said it had been unaffected. Most authorities (59 per cent) believe that the changes have led to an improvement of work planning procedures; only 18 per cent believe they have had a detrimental effect.

Loss of Employment

In January 1987 the union-financed Labour Research Department (LRD) estimated the gross loss of public-service jobs from competitive tendering up to 1986, in the civil service, the NHS and local government, as 71,228. This figure includes both full-time and part-time jobs. The gross loss from contracting out was put at 58,978, and the net loss from contracting out (after allowing for the numbers employed by contractors) as 21,750; the in-house loss was estimated to be 12,250 (PPP, 1987, pp. 6-7 & 46-47). Even if correct, the net figures are small in relation to the millions of people employed by the NHS and local government. Moreover, given the inefficiency of many authorities (as revealed by Audit Commission studies), it is likely that there was considerable over-staffing in some areas—an aspect not much considered by the LRD.

In 1990 a survey by the LRD, based on contracts awarded in the first two rounds of CCT (August 1989 and January 1990), found that 53 per cent of contracts resulted in job losses, 12 per cent produced cuts in pay and 17 per cent cuts in hours. Of contracts won by DSOs, 26 per cent kept jobs, pay and conditions intact; but three-quarters resulted in some loss (SLG, 1990). From the viewpoint of the public-sector unions, it is understandable if gross job losses matter more than net losses, although the distinction is not always clear in references to 'job losses'.

In the 1988/89 *Local Government Chronicle* survey, 300 councils reported some 160 contracts worth £251 million, and the total number of redundancies reported was 1,968. In the following year, 231 authorities reported 476 contracts worth £1,597 million, and 7,376 redundancies were reported, although again the figures might not correspond to the same contracts. Several councils emphasised that most employees so affected had been re-engaged by the new contractor (LGC89; LGC90).

Pay and Conditions

The pay and conditions situation is more complicated. As already mentioned, in the INLOGOV survey the main reason given for changed costs subsequent to tendering was changed productivity, while changed pay levels were mentioned 10 times as reducing costs and six times as increasing them.

The evidence on employees' losses and gains is mixed. In one of the Audit Commission's studies it is noted (November 1990) that operatives in London's building maintenance DLOs work shorter hours and have longer holidays than those working for private contractors. However, their bonus earnings have generally been limited to around £60 a week, giving earnings of just over £200 a week, compared with reported earnings in the private sector of £300 a week or more (AC90d, sections 22 & 38). In their Scottish survey, Kerley and Wynn state that

> 'we have to observe that the best of the private contractors seem able to bid for local authority services on the basis of high productivity, and yet pay wages at least comparable to those negotiated in the NJC' (National Joint Councils).

On the other hand, they also point out that

> 'Services most at risk from tendering are those where the labour costs are a high proportion of overall costs, and where the locally prevailing private sector pay rates for the categories of staff employed, are significantly below those negotiated for DSO workforces' (Kerley and Wynn, 1990, pp. 16 & 36).

In some cases not usually covered by CCT, councils have had to contract out work because their pay scales were insufficiently attractive to potential employees. Nevertheless, it seems that, rather more often than not, council employees, particularly manual workers, have enjoyed better pay and conditions overall than those who have not benefited from such generous employers. Whether one of local authorities' roles should be the redistribution of wealth from the community in general to their employees in particular is at least open to question.

Clients' Costs

A consequence of competition has been a relative reduction in employee costs, according to the INLOGOV study. As a proportion of total costs on both client and contractor sides, employee costs fell from 60 per cent before competition to 56 per cent after it. Premises and capital costs rose from about 30 to about 34 per cent, and central costs from about 9 to about 10 per cent. These changes reflect both reductions in employee levels and increases in capital investment (Walsh, K., 1991, p. 129).

Preparing for competition has involved considerable costs in measuring work, preparing specifications, and so on. Many authorities said they could not separate out these costs, but 10 authorities were able to give figures covering 27 service areas.[1] The average first-time preparation cost in these cases was 10·7 per cent of annual contract size, falling to about 2·5 per cent as a proportion of total contract value. Much of the preparation

---

[1] Few authorities provided figures for the cost of services, before and after competition, broken down by their client and contractor sides. The client/contractor split did not exist previously, so costs were not analysed accordingly. However, some figures were available, and these show an increase in client costs in 16 cases

[Cont'd. on p. 88]

work—estimated by officers interviewed as about 50-60 per cent of the cost—will not, however, need to be repeated for future contracts (Walsh, K., 1991, p. 130).

In the Centre for Business Strategy's study of refuse collection, it was found that cost savings from competitive tendering were on average 20 per cent, but that after the first year of the contract savings averaged 25 per cent. On the other hand, in the first year of operation of a contract the level of savings was 10 per cent, which might suggest that setting-up costs are roughly half of a year's savings (TT, 1990, p. 29). In the *Local Government Chronicle* survey for 1988/89, the cost of monitoring was reported as £3·85 million, an average of £37,000 per contract, and 271 staff (or full-time equivalents) were required, an average of 2·6 per contract (LGC89, p. 8). In a survey by York University in 1984/85, reported by Hartley and Huby, local authorities (in England) replied that the costs of tendering, taking into account the man-hours spent in organising the competition, preparing specifications, site visits and analysing the tenders, averaged £10,000. Usually the time taken to complete the tendering process was about five months. By comparison, firms' costs for tendering were estimated as £4,000 to £5,000 in competing for local authority contracts (but £1,000 to £3,000 when bidding for NHS contracts) (Hartley and Huby, 1985, p. 24).

Discovering the Consumer

Neither competitive tendering nor even contracting out takes away the responsibility of local authorities for the services concerned. In practice the tendering process draws attention to an aspect of their work which has often been neglected— provision of the services that consumers want.[1] As the Local Government Information Unit has

---

out of 24, with no change in four cases, and a decrease in four cases. The average rise in costs, quoted in the study, was 36 per cent (Walsh, K., p. 131). However, a simple average such as this is heavily affected by extreme cases, and in this study the smallest of the 24 costs (which before competition ranged from £8,000 to over £1·6 million) happened to rise the most (by 475 per cent). Total client costs for the 24 cases rose by 13·8 per cent. On the contractor side costs fell in 15 of the 24 cases, and rose in nine cases. Total contractor costs for the 24 cases fell by 8·6 per cent.

[1] As was pointed out by Maurice Healy and Jenny Potter at a conference organised by the National Consumer Council:

'For too long, professionals have had a monopoly in the process of determining "needs". They have tended to assume that they know what sort of services people want; and if they do not actually know what people want, they assume they know what is best for them' (Healy and Potter, 1987, p. 17).

The emphasis which competitive tendering lays on the role of the consumer is emphasised by Norman Flynn and Kieron Walsh.

acknowledged: 'Improving the way councils relate to their users should have been a priority for years. In some areas it has been, in others it has been neglected' (CL, p. 4). Kerley and Wynn observe that, in Scotland at least but probably more generally, there has been a strong tendency for councils of all political opinions to concentrate much more of their efforts on the contracting than on the client side of their functions since 'providing services to the public is seen as synonymous with providing jobs within the authority'. They point out that

'Scottish local authorities were so overwhelmingly concerned with the protection of direct employment in the transition to contracted services, that their major organisational effort in the initial tranches was on the "contractor" side to the detriment of their "client" functions. ... Client side problems have arisen precisely because of the emphasis on maintaining a contracting organisation rather than providing a service' (Kerley and Wynn, 1990, pp. 12 & 29).

In a survey of 235 local authorities by PA Consulting Group and the *Local Government Chronicle*, it was found that 50 per cent carry out no regular reporting of service outputs, and only two in five authorities conduct surveys of what their customers or consumers think of the services provided. Only 16 per cent say that they systematically evaluate the impact of services on the community. Only 7 per cent of authorities had introduced 'quality circles' and only 6 per cent had introduced 'quality programmes'. Less than half listen to ideas from their employees. However, 70 per cent say they share 'best practice' with other local authorities (PA, pp. 12-13).

Quality of Services

In a comparative study of council services in several countries, *It Can All Be Done Better*, David Green, Director of Works with Sheffield City Council, writes:

'Comparisons between Britain and the USA, Canada, France and Denmark show conclusively that in services such as street cleansing, refuse collection, amenity area maintenance (verges and the like) our standards are appalling and nowhere near as good as they should—and regrettably, could—be.

'And perhaps surprisingly to many, the reasons are not difficult to find, nor is the main reason "lack of money". Yes—more cash would help but it also boils down to past concentration on cost reduction instead of quality (particularly by the Audit Commission),[1] lack of will, initiative and

---

[1] This criticism of the Audit Commission does not appear to be justified. John Banham, then Controller of the Audit Commission, observed in 1985 that 'the need to define standards of service to be provided and to monitor performance closely must be considered before contracts are even put out to tender' (Supplement to *Local Government Chronicle*, 5 July 1985, p. twelve).

investment in research and development, low expectations both by the provider and the public, poor management, inadequacies in local government information and administration, and seemingly an acceptance that the Country shouldn't expect anything better' (Green, 1990, sections 3.1-3.2).

The purpose of competitive tendering is improvement in value for money, resulting in lower cost, improved quality or some measure of both.[1] At times the objective of maintaining or improving quality might have been overlooked in the enthusiasm for making savings, but these are judgements for individual authorities in the light of local and current circumstances—the decision is theirs.

While supporters of contracting out have produced lists of the great savings claimed as resulting from competitive tendering (PSR), opponents of contracting out have catalogued the many failings they believe have been discovered in the work done by private contractors, though these appear to have been mainly in the period when councils and contractors were still learning to understand each other (MCF).The Public Services Privatisation Research Unit claims that the evidence from more than 5,000 contracts shows that the failure rate of contracts held by private contractors is four and a half times higher than for contracts held by the in-house workforce in local government (and 18 times higher in the health service) (*Public Service Action*, July 1992, p. 8).

One critic of CCT writes that 'initial opposition to local government privatisation in the early 1980s was focused around the inadequacies of the service provided by private contractors', but he goes on to acknowledge: 'However, with the greater emphasis that is now being placed on specification and monitoring procedures this may prove to be less of a problem in the future' (Painter, 1990, p. 19). Furthermore he points out that 'Some authorities have used the [contract] specification to raise the standards of service currently being provided' (Painter, 1990, p. 6). This is confirmed by INLOGOV's survey, discussed above, in which changing standards were mentioned much more often as increasing costs than as reducing them. If competitive tendering is used to obtain better value for money, then it is for councils to decide whether to provide the same level of service and quality at reduced cost, or better quality at the same cost, or some other combination of these features.

---

[1] When, in February 1987, Christopher Chope, junior Environment Minister, spoke of the then forthcoming legislation he stressed that, although savings were expected, '. . . the emphasis must be on value for money, not the lowest price' (Winetrobe and Nield, 1987, p. 7).

The introduction of competition has required an examination of standards of service for inclusion in contract specifications. This has been beneficial since in many cases previous standards have not been explicit or even ascertainable. Owing largely to competition, there has been a growing interest in quality assessment and management. Some critics of competition have pointed to the increased costs which contract supervision and management entail; they seem to assume that DSOs can automatically provide quality without the need for much, if any, supervision. This assumption has been shown by the work of the Audit Commission to be false.[1]

The key stages in ensuring satisfactory quality are:

(i)   contract specifications which accurately reflect the council's objectives;

(ii)   careful selection of contractor;

(iii)   good monitoring throughout the term of the contract.

These should apply whether or not contracting out is used. It should not be assumed, as is often implied, that the existing level of a service, in terms of either quality or quantity, is necessarily the right one. It might be either too low or too high.[2]

Monitoring of Services

One of the costs associated with competitive tendering, and particularly with contracting out, is that of monitoring the quantity and quality of the work done by contractors. However, it is not only one of the costs but also one of the benefits of competitive tendering that it has encouraged authorities to take more seriously something which they have hitherto neglected, presumably on the basis that services which they provided directly did not need to be assessed in detail. One reason for this neglect must have been that

---

[1] The Commission rightly comments that

'For most types of work, client supervision will certainly need to improve to meet the challenges of CCT; this should not, however, be seen as a cost of CCT but rather the belated addressing of a major management weakness' (AC89a, p. 18).

[2] John Zetter of the OECD has observed that, as a result of budgetary pressure,

'governments at all levels are searching for new ways to increase the efficiency of urban services and, in some cases, to reduce the quality or quantity of service provided either due to changing priorities or because certain standards are considered to be unnecessarily high' (Zetter, 1984, p. 52).

Priorities can, and should, change but value for money should always be sought. For example, in a study in the United States, as we see later (below, p. 136), it was found that residents tended to prefer a reduced level of service at lower cost.

no alternative contractor was normally envisaged, even as a remote possibility.

The Audit Commission stated in 1988 that

'The need to monitor results better is universally accepted in local government—the problem is that few councils do it very well, and some scarcely do it at all. In the Commission's view, it is the function that most authorities do least well and should be the easiest to correct. The real difficulty in measuring or monitoring some aspects of council services is no excuse for failure to monitor those results that easily can be measured' (AC88a, p. 8).

The Commission points out that council members should play a key role in monitoring and appraising performance, but that most councils' management arrangements do little to promote this (AC88a, p. 9).

In a study of the way in which council members spend their time, the Commission found that, while authorities vary greatly, in general 'reviewing past performance accounts for an insignificant proportion of members' time'. Moreover,

'many service committees seem to focus almost exclusively on organisational issues and inputs—how much money is spent, the terms and conditions under which people are employed—rather than on the results achieved in terms of services delivered and, crucially, the quality of those services' (AC90b, pp. 6-7).

The INLOGOV study found that, for refuse collection, three out of 12 authorities which had let contracts had had no explicit process of inspection before the impact of competition, whereas all said they would have such a process subsequently. Only three had had dedicated inspectors before competition, against nine which intended to use them afterwards. For street cleaning, out of nine authorities only one had had an explicit process of monitoring before competition, compared with eight after competition. Monitoring methods also changed. Instead of the general use of visual judgements, a major impact of competition was found to be the development of explicit written standards for most services (Walsh, K., 1991, p. 143).

Whether the work of DSOs is monitored as keenly as that of outside contractors is a question which does not feature strongly, if at all, in surveys of competitive tendering. In their Scottish survey, Kerley and Wynn state that local authority staff

'are now making the assumption that monitoring should be as rigorously applied to a successful internal contractor as to an external firm. However, we are not necessarily persuaded that the strict demands of the client side role will be adhered to rigorously and impartially by all councils' (Kerley and Wynn, 1990, p. 25).

Contract Failure

Information on the failure of contracts was collected as part of the Local Government Management Board's survey covering 3,475 contracts in England and Wales. Of 46 contracts terminated for reasons other than 'Section 14' notices, 21 terminations were in ground maintenance, eight in building cleaning, seven in refuse collection, six in catering (other), three in vehicle maintenance, and one in other cleaning. Of the total, 14 were held by DSOs, and a few by management buy-out companies. Of those awarded to private contractors, some were terminated because the contractor went out of business. Larger numbers of contracts resulted in financial penalties. For example, in building cleaning 55 contracts led to penalties (the highest being over £16,000), split almost equally between DSOs and private contractors (CCTIS, 1991, pp. 10 & 17).

Allegations of widespread failure by private contractors have formed a noticeable part of campaigns against competitive tendering by the Trades Union Congress, several trade unions and organisations sponsored by them (MCF; PCPC; RC; TTCL). That some contracts have been failures cannot be disputed. The problem arose largely through inexperience on the part both of contractors in tendering for and doing new types of work, and of councils in issuing specifications and in assessing tenders and tenderers. It is not a problem confined to private contractors, and it appears to have diminished considerably as both sides have gained experience. Even a publication about CCT in the refuse and street cleaning markets, produced in 1990 by opponents of CCT, states of the contractors that 'Their strategies are now more sophisticated and their understanding both of the service and the market much clearer' (RC, p. 30). In the United States too, it was noted some years ago that the success of 'privatisation' would probably remain hampered for a while until the public and private sectors got more used to dealing with each other (Seader, 1986, p. 6).

An inevitable conclusion about contract failure is that arrived at by Howard Davies, then Controller of the Audit Commission:

'If contractors have given a bad service, what we are really saying is that the council has chosen badly, has not specified its contracts properly or has not monitored them properly, because these client functions do remain firmly the responsibility of local authorities and it is quite wrong to argue that councillors lose their responsibilities for these services. Their responsibility must be implemented in a different sort of way but they are still responsible ...' (Davies, p. 21).

Contract Size and Length

Among the provisions of the legislation relating to anti-competitive behaviour, the size and packaging of contracts are of importance. The size of contracts varies very considerably, with some— especially those for school catering and refuse collection which most authorities have chosen not to sub-divide—amounting to millions of pounds. Even where they have been sub-divided, the majority of school catering contracts are still for millions of pounds; moreover, many contractors have argued that it is not logistically possible for them to start a contract in possibly hundreds of sites all on the same day (Mark Pollard, 'Food for Thought', *Municipal Journal*, 15 March 1991, p. 33). Contracts which are very large prevent all but the largest contractors from being able to participate. In some other areas, authorities have offered smaller contracts by dividing the work into smaller packages.

Some authorities have combined different services into single contracts, and this could either be mutually convenient for the authority and the contractor, or a way of making the package unattractive for specialised businesses to undertake. For example, street cleaning and refuse collection are sometimes combined, or the provision of a service combined with maintenance of vehicles used in providing that service. Similarly, the management of leisure facilities might be combined with the associated catering and cleaning.

The overall strategy of the 40 authorities surveyed by INLOGOV has been to let large single-purpose contracts which reflect their present patterns of organisation and management of the work. Partly because of this, but even more because of the wide variation in size of local authorities, the range of contract size is very large. The average size of contracts for ground maintenance was £285,000 (with a range of £25,000 to £1 million), whereas the average for school and welfare catering was about £2 million (with a range of £373,000 to over £13 million) (Walsh, K., 1991, p. 30).

Table 7 gives average and maximum sizes of contracts for different services as reported by the LGMB, and maximum sizes given by the IPF, in surveys published early in 1992. The LGMB survey covers only England and Wales, while the IPF one includes also Scotland. All figures are for annual values of contracts, not for total values, and the averages have been expressed in millions of pounds instead of thousands. The figures for refuse collection include those for refuse collection and other (street) cleaning combined.

Authorities have usually let single contracts for all their refuse

Table 7:
Average and Maximum Annual Value of Contracts for Different Services, 1988 to 1992*

Service	Ave. (LGMB)	Max. (LGMB) £ million	Max. (IPF)
Building cleaning	0·43	7·3	>18
Refuse collection, of which	1·37	8·0	>12
Refuse collection and other cleaning combined	1·94	. . .	. . .
Other cleaning	0·48	5·3	8
Vehicle maintenance	0·46	3·5	>4
Catering (education and welfare)	1·86	12·8	13·6
Catering (other)	0·16	1·7	2·8
Ground maintenance	0·30	4·1	3·7
Sports and leisure management	0·63	6·8	. . .

. . . = not available or not applicable.

*As for Tables 1 (CCTIS) and 5 (McGuirk).

Source: CCTIS (1991), pp. 8, 14, 21, 24, 28, 34, 38, 44, 52 & 55; McGuirk (1992), pp. 10, 17, 25, 33, 41, 43 & 50.

collection and street cleaning, partly because this is the way they organise these types of work. Contracts for ground maintenance and building cleaning, on the other hand, are usually separated on a geographical basis, and this is reflected to some extent in smaller average contract sizes. Voluntary organisations are particularly likely to be concerned about the size of contracts.[1]

---

[1] As Kunz, Jones and Spencer write:

'Voluntary organisations need to have an interest in pointing out that small contracts may often serve the interests of a local community better. They will enable contractors to take better account of specific circumstances and will provide more direct links between contractors and the community served. Very importantly, small contracts will allow the community to get together to try to bid for running the services themselves, in particular in cases where they are not satisfied with current services. . . .

'Small contracts promote fuller competition in that they allow comparisons between different contractors and approaches in similar circumstances. This opens the door to alternative forms of service delivery which may prove to be better but would not have been tried otherwise. From the point of view of the community the greater range and variety of services on offer will increase the element of choice' (Kunz et al., 1989, p. 26).

Table 8:
Maximum, Minimum and Average Lengths of Contracts Awarded for Different Services, 1988 to 1991*

Service	Minimum	Maximum	Average*
		Length in years	
Building cleaning	3 or 4	4 or 6	3·7
Refuse collection	5	7	5·1
Other cleaning	4	6	4·4
Vehicle maintenance	4	6	4·6
Catering (education and welfare	4	5 or 6	4·3
Catering (other)	4	6	4·4
Ground maintenance	3 or 4	4 or 6	4·0
Sports and leisure management	4	6	4·6

*The averages (in col. 3) apply to the period between the implementation of the 1988 Act and the publication of CCTIS in April 1991.

Source: CCTIS (1991), p. 8.

Contracts generally run for periods of from three to seven years, depending on the service and the type of authority (AC89a, p. 11). The regulations set minimum and maximum periods within which authorities may choose.[1] The LGMB study found that contract lengths are generally near the low end of the permitted ranges. Statutory minima and maxima, and the actual averages for different services, are as shown in Table 8. Very similar averages are reported by the Institute of Public Finance (McGuirk, 1992).

Contracts for periods which are too long are undesirable because of the delay in replacing an unsatisfactory contractor and the risk that a contractor may become complacent. The traditional reliance of councils on in-house contractors which never had to face competition had the disadvantage that in effect the contracts were indefinitely long, and the in-house contractors could become correspondingly complacent. On the other hand, contracts which are too short can increase costs because the client must go through the tendering procedures more often, and because start-up costs are written off over a shorter period. In addition, there is

---

[1] In some cases these vary according to whether or not authorities have education functions, the lower figures applying to those which do have education functions (LGAC, para. 39).

less opportunity for the client and contractor to get to know each other.

Competition and Contract Size

Among the reasons for which local authorities make contracts the size they are, the nature of the work and administrative convenience both play a part. In view of the attitude of many councils to contracting out, however, there must also be a suspicion that making contracts as large, or as small, as possible is one of the various methods employed to discourage private bidders. Indeed, already in 1987 the Audit Commission observed that it was 'aware of attempts to avoid the necessity for DLOs to compete, by packaging work in such a way that no local supplier is likely to be able to compete for the contract'. It added that

'Such stratagems amount to deliberate destruction of local value—because the supposed interests of DLO employees are placed above those of the authority's customers or its ratepayers.' (AC87, p. 7)

The Commission has recommended that standing orders should specify that services be put out to tender in lots of not more than £50,000 (about the annual cost of cleaning and caretaking for a comprehensive school) (AC87, p. 7). On the other hand, it has also written that 'authority-wide refuse collection contracts have proved attractive to the private sector in the past and are unlikely to be anti-competitive' (AC89a, p. 12). In practice, SCAT reported that virtually all such contracts let in the first year were for authority-wide packages; many were for street cleaning and refuse collection combined, and these had an average value of £2·07 million (RC, p. 25).

The practice of making contracts as large as many have been is often anti-competitive, either in the sense of making it difficult to find private contractors able to offer an alternative to the larger DSOs, or in the sense of making much of the work suitable only for the largest private contractors. The INLOGOV study observes that for building cleaning, smaller contracts were more likely to attract bids (Walsh, K., 1991, p. 139). Tom McGuirk points out in relation to vehicle maintenance that the annual average size of contracts has risen, and that local contractors have consistently complained that the funding required to handle projects of this size tends to exclude all but the larger companies. Ground maintenance contracts are considered too large by many companies who would like to see them broken down into manageable sizes. Many catering contractors are put off from bidding for school catering by several factors, including the very large size of contracts and the numerous sites involved. School cleaning contracts also tend to be large, and to stay in-house (McGuirk, 1992, pp. 22, 30, 39 & 47). The failure of some authorities to divide contracts into manageable sizes has led in extreme cases to some government warnings (described, with reference to the 1988 Act, as 'section 13 notices').[1]

The Audit Commission has pointed out that to let a number of contracts with separate tenders for each is one way of fostering competition in some services. It suggests:

'Although it should not be deliberately engineered, it might be fortuitous if two or three different contractors were engaged, since this would avoid the authority being prey to a monopoly supplier' (AC89a, p. 13).

More importantly, the Commission proposes that authorities approach contractors to ascertain the type of contracts likely to generate most interest, and the size of contracts with which they are able to cope. To do so would be in the best interests of securing value for money.[2] It is not evident, however, that many authorities follow this advice.

Economies of Scale

A possible justification for very large contracts could be based on economies of scale associated with the types of work involved. However, the Audit Commission has stated that

'none of the Commission's studies has so far revealed any large economies of scale in respect of local authority functions; indeed, there is circumstantial evidence of managerial diseconomies of scale' (AC87, p. 7).

A study of refuse collection by the Centre for Business Strategy at London Business School found that 'there are no significant economies or diseconomies of scale' (TT, 1990, p. 27). In the United States, Robert Poole goes further, again with regard to refuse collection:

'There are very few economies of scale. In fact, as city sanitation departments demonstrate, there are more often *diseconomies* of scale— that is, rising unit costs as size increases, due to ever-increasing administrative costs. When garbage service is unregulated, as in sprawling Los Angeles County, the number of firms rapidly proliferates' (Poole, 1980, p. 90).

---

[1] For example, a notice was issued to Liverpool city council over a multi-million-pound ground maintenance contract awarded in-house (Pollard, 1990).

[2] It may also be a legal requirement. Fox Williams point out that there must be an onus on authorities to conduct some degree of market research into the ability of relevant contractors to deliver the service which they are contemplating exposing to competition (CCTLGA, 1991, p. 24).

Poole states that the size of a town, in terms of area and population, is unlikely to be the optimum for most services. For some services it might be more efficient for several towns, especially if they are small, to be covered by a single supplier, while for other services a town, especially if it is large, might be better served by several suppliers (Poole, 1983). For this reason autarkic direct provision, to which many local authorities cling, could be inherently wasteful, quite apart from the question of competition.

Furthermore, even if there were significant economies of scale, they could and should be discovered by experience rather than conveniently assumed to exist. As the Commission points out, one way of ensuring the best result is to break work up into three or four parcels, and allow contractors to bid for one or more as they see fit.

'Each will then be able to select the mix which it finds most attractive. Bids should then reflect any economies of scale while the authority will be able to select the offers which give it the lowest overall price' (AC89a, p. 14).

If local government were to become more truly local, this would tend to lead to smaller contracts.[1] Meanwhile, more needs to be done about the problem of excessively large contracts.

Local Authority Management

CCT does not alter the statutory duties and responsibilities of local authorities. It should, however, alter their way of working and their management structure. As a general rule authorities need to separate clearly their functions as client and as contractor, and to structure their departments and management accordingly.[2] The attention of councillors and senior officers ought to be concentrated more on matters of effectiveness and quality (AC89a, p. 3).

---

[1] A factor which could help is the growing realisation that large-scale 'local' government is a mistake. The Audit Commission caught this mood when it wrote that one

'basic assumption now under challenge is that services are best provided by big centralised authorities, with the ability to employ a suitably professional organisation, and to co-ordinate activities on a large scale. . . . Thinking here has also changed. It is recognised that large size also has disadvantages: loss of responsiveness, loss of local initiative, and sometimes excessive administration costs—factors which can more than offset the advantages of large size' (AC88a, p. 4).

[2] Clarke and Stewart distinguish not two but three functions: 'the client role (what service is to be provided at what level), the contract management role (setting the contract and monitoring it) and managing the contractor—in-house or external' (Clarke and Stewart, 1989a, p. 4).

Restructuring

The introduction of competition requires a radical change in the attitudes of local authority officers and members, and in procedures and structures. A survey by PA Consulting Group and the *Local Government Chronicle* in late 1989 received a response from 235 councils. They found that

'a number of authorities have restructured to reflect the dramatically changing political and managerial agenda. The traditional local authority with its emphasis on hierarchical and professional interests, often with a strong legal and accountancy bias, is under increasing threat.... Some 9 out of 10 local authorities say they have restructured as a number of services have been subjected to competition in the market place.'

Some seven in 10 authorities were found to have established separate committees for contracting activities and a clear contractor/client split. Only half the authorities said they had a corporate strategic plan, and only 36 per cent plan more than one year ahead (PA, pp. 5, 8-9, 11).

In INLOGOV's survey, it was found that 'The general attitude of those interviewed was that change would take a long time because attitudes and basic values and approaches were difficult to change' (Walsh, K., 1991, pp. 26-27). In their Scottish survey, Kerley and Wynn note that

'A consistent theme in our discussions with local authority officers was that the structural implications of CCT ... have led to a necessary shift *from control to facilitation* on the part of the traditionally dominant central service departments.[1] ... Most agreed ... that the impact of CCT had significantly altered the balance of influence within their authority, away from the central departments' (Kerley and Wynn, 1990, pp. 14 & 34).

Client and Contractor Roles

A survey of client/contractor relationships was undertaken by the Local Government Management Board between July and December 1991. Information was collected from 284 authorities in England and Wales (CCRR, 1992, pp. 3 & 5). The most common arrangement found on the client side is for all four functions—contract preparation, tendering process, tender evaluation, and contract management—to be carried out by the same department. However, there are other arrangements, such as preparation of contracts by individual departments, tendering supervision by a specialist unit, and contract management by a lead client department.

---

[1] Some council officers are so concerned about the potential for disruption of corporate decision-making structures that one seminar participant claimed that ' *"DSOs are the Rottweilers of the local government world"*—fine if they do what you ask, potentially beyond your control and dangerous if they have other urges' (Kerley and Wynn, 1990, p. 34).

Service delivery is most commonly provided by a multi-functional DSO, although significant numbers have other arrangements. In sports and leisure management, however, it is more common for client and contractor units to be within the same department. In the case of members' committees, there is a greater separation of responsibilities, and a majority of authorities have separate committees for the client and contractor sides.

The client role is that of setting service standards, preparing contracts, inviting and evaluating tenders, and monitoring the work of contractors. The contractor role is that of tendering for and carrying out the work of contracts. The Audit Commission has stated that it believes strongly in a clear separation between the client and contractor roles within an authority, and that authorities should develop new organisational structures to create that separation. Clients should be concerned with service standards and value for money, while contractors should be concerned with winning contracts and performing to standard and price. Among the reasons given for separation are that it clarifies the differing objectives of each role, that the in-house contractor is more likely to operate effectively, and that it will demonstrate that the authority is serious about giving equal treatment to all contractors. The Commission found that it was the small authorities which were mainly in the vanguard of full separation by putting client and contractor into different departments. Many of the larger authorities, particularly metropolitan districts and London boroughs, were retaining mixed departments (AC88b, pp. 16 & 18; AC89a, p. 6).

An indication of why authorities have behaved differently in this respect is given by Richard Kerley and Douglas Wynn in their Scottish survey:

'One generalisation which may be supportable, though, is that the thoroughness with which the client/contractor division is enforced within authorities, depends crucially on the political aspirations of those authorities—the more relative weight the authority wishes to give to the maintenance of public sector employment (and being a "good employer" in particular) the less rigorously will the division be drawn. . . . Scottish authorities have apparently acted within the imprecise terms of the 1988 Act, but the intention of the majority and of COSLA was unquestionably to use the maximum discretion which they believed they had, to assist the "in-house" teams to win their contracts, and this in the main they achieved' (Kerley and Wynn, 1990, p. 11).

Benefits of Competition

Steve Evans has seen 'three major benefits being imparted by competition: clarification of policies;[1] reductions in unit costs; and changes to the structure of authorities which go hand-in-hand with a more businesslike approach' (TT, 1990, p. 18). David Parker observes that

> 'In raising efficiency, competitive tendering appears to be achieving what other reforms such as programme budgeting, management by objectives and efficiency audits failed to achieve over the last decade or so' (Parker, 1990b, p. 666).

Tom McGuirk remarks, in connection with refuse collection, that

> 'regardless of the increased costs or savings, the major benefit deriving from CCT has been the definition of service standards as set out in contract specifications which largely did not exist prior to the introduction of the competitive tendering legislation' (McGuirk, 1992, p. 5).

One of the fears which councils had of contracting out was that it would diminish their control over the service concerned.[2] However, Robert Poole in the United States, with nine years' experience of local governments in seven states, asserts that

> 'Many local officials find that a private supplier under contract is far more responsive and concerned about the quality of service than municipal personnel who take it for granted that they will be providing the service in perpetuity' (Poole, 1983).

Direct Service Organisations

There can be little doubt that the in-house works departments now known as direct service organisations (DSOs) have been greatly

---

[1] On policy clarification, Evans points out that this is one of the more lasting benefits:
'For too long, authorities have muddled along without any clear statement—and in some cases without even a clear understanding—of what they are trying to get out of a service. And what CCT is forcing them to do is to re-appraise the objectives of their service and in effect to put the service under the magnifying glass and to force them to re-appraise the service in a way that they have not done before, and to make decisions that they have not taken before.' (TT, 1990, p. 18).

[2] Mike Blundy is among those who have pointed out that the advantage is more likely to be the other way. Even allowing for his position with a private contractor, and a somewhat rosy vision, his comments are relevant:
'Better and quicker resource control can be achieved quite easily when you have a private contractor in place. . . . With a private contractor in place you will get more rapid response than with the DLO, simply because he has very short lines of communication, a very short decision-making process, and more delegation of authority. He has a reputation to protect and will do what you require. Many of the local authorities who have got private contractors in place remark that they have actually achieved greater flexibility. You can demand what you want, when you want, and you can discuss changes in workload without causing yourself political problems' (TT, 1990, p. 54).

improved as a direct result of CCT. At a conference in 1986, held to discuss the prospect of CCT, 'there was general agreement that councils and unions could best defend their position by co-operating to provide efficient, well-marketed services which were understood and valued by the public'. One speaker acknowledged that the possibility of legislation had forced a situation which should have been the case anyway—that local authorities were beginning to manage their services properly. It was generally recognised in the ensuing discussion that it had been the Green Paper (*Competition in the Provision of Local Authority Services*, February 1985) which had had the beneficial effect of forcing councils to examine their operations (PCR, pp. 17 & 20). In January 1989 the *Financial Times* commented that 'many councils have improved efficiency so markedly that in many cases they should be able to repulse private competition and continue to use direct labour' (Parker, 1990a, p. 14).

Some aspects of the effect of competitive tendering on direct service organisations are among those affecting the management of authorities. The separation of contractor and client roles is a fundamental element of change affecting DSOs, as is the need to operate in a competitive environment.[1] The INLOGOV study indicates that DSOs have changed in several ways. The degree of delegation to DSO managers has increased. In most cases the pressures of competition have led to improved teamwork and improved morale, particularly at the management level. In many cases new work disciplines have been introduced as a result of a conscious effort to reduce lost time and to deal with problems of excessive and persistent absenteeism, a move normally strongly supported by the majority of the workforce. There is a stronger sense of solidarity with others in the DSO, and a commitment to be seen to be doing a good-quality job (Walsh, K., 1991, pp. 68-71). Keith Hartley has suggested that some, if not all, of any budget savings made by a DSO, subsequent to a successful tender bid, should accrue to the staff of the in-house unit which would then have every incentive to operate as a worker co-operative (Hartley, 1984, p. 14).

An ironic consequence of CCT, noted by Kerley and Wynn in Scotland, has been that DSOs have been forced to consider the cost of the support services they receive within their authorities.

---

[1] Clarke and Stewart state that 'A DSO tied to the traditional pattern of committee working would soon be ineffective and incapable of taking decisions with the speed required to provide a competitive service' (Clarke, 1989a, p. 7).

This is beginning to have the result that some DSOs are asking for the freedom to buy from external suppliers some of the services they need.[1]

Management Buy-Outs

One consequence of competitive tendering even before it became compulsory has been a small movement towards sale of direct-labour or service departments to their managers. Management buy-outs (MBOs) can have the advantage of their managers and employees retaining their former work. In addition, managers acquire greater responsibility and a stake in their own business, while all concerned obtain the freedom to seek work not available to DSOs. Most of the MBOs set up by local authorities in defined services or CCT areas have also offered some degree of share ownership to employees (Paddon, 1991, p. 29). For the council there is the advantage of being free to concentrate on the role of an 'enabler' rather than a 'provider' of the services concerned. Some councils also see a benefit in being able to award contracts to their former employees without using competitive tendering (which is compulsory only where a contract is given to an in-house department).

By early 1990 there had been only about 10 management buy-outs, though most were on a large scale. Some of the resulting firms were unprofitable and have folded, while others have succeeded not only in retaining council work but also in gaining contracts from the private sector (Parker, 1990a, p. 13; Paine, 1984). It appears that MBOs are more likely to be considered at the extreme ends of the spectrum of viability: either where there is a bleak future for the DSO anyway, due to intense local competition, or where the prospect of success is particularly favourable (Howes and Inglis, 1991, p. 24). According to the Local Government Information Unit, MBO firms are typically sold by the buy-out

---

[1] 'The development of internal markets for support services therefore, and somewhat ironically, is tending to empower managers of contracted public services, in their role as clients of the central departments.' Moreover,

'Ideally, from the perspective of the DSO manager, the authority would provide a properly costed "menu" of support services, indicate which elements are for compulsory consumption and which are discretionary, and which may be purchased from external suppliers.'

They point out also that

'Managers will have to take greater direct operational responsibility for their DSO, instead of allowing the diffusion of responsibility (or blame for errors) which characterises the present complex and hierarchical structures of local authority decision making' (Kerley and Wynn, 1990, pp. 14 & 35).

team after between two and four years of being started. The business is most likely to be sold to a company trying to enter, or seeking to expand within, the local authority market, though some are floated publicly. The Unit adds: 'Significantly over 10 per cent go into receivership' (MBOLG, 1991, p. 4).

FIVE

Central Government and the National Health Service

In this chapter we look at the impact of competitive tendering on central government, and in particular on the Ministry of Defence. The development of tendering for auxiliary services in the National Health Service, and its results, are examined, and some of the arguments for and against it are presented. Lastly, the scope for extending competition in the health service is discussed.

Central Government

Government policies, so far as central government departments and the National Health Service are concerned, can generally be implemented by administrative action and thus do not require legislation. In 1986 a report was published of a multi-departmental review of competitive tendering and contracting-out for services in government departments (HMT, 1986). This Report was commissioned jointly by the Chief Secretary to the Treasury and the Prime Minister's Adviser on Efficiency, with the objective of extending the application of the Government's policy on the use of competition in the provision of departmental services and improving the ways in which the policy was delivered in practice.[1]

The Report was written against a background of a government policy of subjecting as much work as possible to competition and of contracting work out whenever it would be commensurate with sound management and good value for money to do so. The aims of that policy were: reducing the size of the Civil Service; saving money; and increasing the share of the economy in which market forces can operate. In this it differs from CCT as applied to local authorities, where the emphasis has been solely on obtaining better value for money.

The Report states that 'competitive tendering' means testing the

---

[1] The Ministry of Agriculture, Fisheries and Food, the Ministry of Defence, the Department of Energy, the Home Office, the Property Services Agency and the Department of Trade and Industry contributed to the review by scrutinising their practices in this matter.

efficiency of in-house services against tenders from outside contractors; 'contracting out' means letting a contract for those services. Contracting out differs from privatisation in that the service in question remains a public service, publicly financed. Ministers or other public authorities continue to decide what service shall be provided to whom, and to be accountable for it.[1]

The Departments' scrutinies showed that pressure of manpower targets had proved the most important motivation, but that different Ministers gave the policy a different emphasis. Furthermore, while the Prime Minister's original policy statement in 1980 was in the context of Civil Service manpower, when the Treasury relaunched the policy in 1984 it was in value-for-money terms, with the emphasis on saving money. It was then seen as one of a range of efficiency measures which would essentially save money, but incidentally help to achieve manpower targets. The Report confirmed this new emphasis.

Range of Activities

The Treasury's list of activities for mandatory competitive tendering was: cleaning, laundry, catering, security guarding, and maintenance work. Activities for which testing was not mandatory but which were 'worth considering' were: messengers, libraries, postal services, and press cuttings. However, in January 1985 the Chief Secretary stated that

'Departments should continue to cast their net as wide as possible so as to ensure that as much work as possible is subject to competition. Every opportunity for competitive tendering, across the widest range of departmental activity, needs to be identified.' (HMT, 1986, p. 16)

The Report went further, recommending that Departments review *all* their activities to see whether they offered scope for contracting out. However, rather than suggesting additions to the Treasury's list of prescribed services, the Report recommended that Departments start to think for themselves what services might be tested by competition. Departments should be required to explain why they are not putting out to tender any service in which a contractor has expressed an interest.

Dialogue with Contractors

Early dialogue is greatly welcomed by contractors, as it saves them much time; it is all too rare for public-sector clients, who

---

[1] The review covered provision by the private sector both of support services within Departments and of services to the public. It excluded contracts for the supply of goods, and contracts of a capital nature.

prefer to stay at arm's length. Several contractors made the point that a relationship with the public sector could work only if the contractor were wanted and not imposed. Contractors often considered that the public sector tends to overspecify, thus restricting their scope for innovation, using economy of scale or employing standard methods and materials. An output-based specification leaves greater flexibility and should provide greater value for money for the public sector.

Managers' Attitudes

The Report found widespread prejudice in the Civil Service against the use of contractors, not only on the part of members of trade unions, who were concerned about employment prospects, but also on the part of managers. There was a managerial presumption that in-house services were best in principle, and that contracting out might save money but only at a price in terms of management control. Managers often had a false sense of security in staying with in-house services, although they had no objective standard by which to judge.[1] However, those who had contracted out successfully did not feel less secure; on the contrary, many felt more in control.

Until there is a contract, it is rare to find an explicit specification for a service in the public sector, and still rarer to find performance and output measures in force. Contractors have to work to the price they specified. An in-house workforce is never subject to the same degree of discipline; if costs overrun, money can be transferred from some other service to supplement the budget, or staff can be used to cover for one another. On the other hand, contracting out is not an easy option, since it places considerable burdens on managers, in addition to their normal work.

Favourable Results

The Report concludes that the Departments' scrutinies

'place it beyond doubt that contracting out is viable over a wide range of activities in government. There is by now a substantial body of experience which demonstrates that it is possible to obtain the standard of service required, to give the contractor a reasonable profit, and to make worthwhile savings at the same time.'

Competitive tendering is improving efficiency by introducing the discipline of drawing up a proper specification, exposing outdated

---

[1] The amount of control exercised by a Civil Service manager was more limited than it seemed, according to the Report. There was no power to 'hire and fire', and the instruments of reward and discipline were remote and imprecise.

Table 9:
Savings Achieved by Contracting-Out:
Actual and Cumulative, 1980-81 to 1985-86

	1980-81	1981-82	1982-83	1983-84	1984-85	1985-86
			£ million			
Actual	0·6	7·5	4·5	3·6	3·7	2·1
Cumulative	0·6	8·1	12·6	16·2	19·9	22·0

Source: HMT (1991), p. 15.

and restrictive practices, and pointing up opportunities to deliver better services at lower cost. Contracting out is yielding savings of money and manpower, while providing satisfactory services (improved services in some cases) and hitherto unexpected advantages in terms of management control.

The Report found that there had been substantial progress in contracting out the basic ancillary services: 84 per cent of cleaning, 82 per cent of maintenance, and 73 per cent of laundry services had been contracted out. However, in general the policy appeared to have lost momentum, and a new impetus was needed. This is illustrated by the savings given in Table 9, although the figures understate the benefit because they do not fully capture the greater efficiency of in-house operations in a competitive situation.

According to the Report, the general rule is that contracting out saves money on ancillary services but is likely to cost more than in-house provision of 'professional' services.[1] Nevertheless, it can still be worthwhile to test such activities through competition. Contractors claim that they possess special expertise and are equipped with the latest technology. Evidence on better technology is patchy. Where the contractors have the edge is in the toughness

---

[1] The Report states that, as a general rule, contracting out saves money among lower-paid staff and costs more among higher-paid staff; most of the savings from contracting out arise because contractors offer poorer conditions of employment. Contractors in the ancillary services usually offer similar basic rates of pay (sometimes less, sometimes a little more), but they eliminate costly bonus schemes and overtime working, provide little if any sick pay, and avoid national insurance payments by means of more part-time working; pensions are the most important factor. The Report states that the Civil Service has always been a 'good employer', and it is right that it should continue to be such, but it hints that the Civil Service has been too good an employer at some levels. It is this departure from market levels of pay and conditions which opens the way for viable contracting out.

of their management.[1] The real potential of the market will only be exploited as the opportunities for work in the Civil Service are made clear, and as Departments go out and make contacts, formal and informal, with potential suppliers. The Public Procurement Policy Guidelines are written in terms of procurement of equipment, but much of what they say about intelligent purchasing 'reads across' to contracting for services. In concluding their main recommendations, the authors of the Report state:

'In our opinion these principles, adjusted as necessary to suit their different circumstances, could be applied also in the National Health Service, in local government and in non-departmental public bodies.'

More recently the Treasury, strengthened since 1986 by a Central Unit on Purchasing, have prepared annual progress reports on purchasing by central government. For 1989-90, government departments reported formal market testing of activities with previous costs of £24·1 million and associated savings of some £5·8 million; some 94 per cent of the work tested was contracted out. In addition, activities carried out by military personnel with a total value of £4·9 million were tested, and savings of £1·6 million were obtained. Cumulative annual savings through market testing in the Civil Service were running at an estimated £54 million (HMT, 1991, p. 45). More detailed information on 'market testing' by individual central government departments is provided in a White Paper issued in November 1991 (CQBB, pp. 8-13 & 26-35).

Proposed Extension

The Financial Secretary to the Treasury, Francis Maude, stated in March 1992 that rigorous application of competitive tendering had delivered average savings in central government of around 25 per cent on pre-testing costs. It is proposed to open up new areas to competition. As a result, departments, executive agencies and non-departmental public bodies will be testing the scope for a greater private-sector contribution to the delivery of services. Possible activities include accounting, auditing, inspection and review, legal services, operational research, project management, payments of grants and subsidies, and advisory services (Maude, 1992, pp. 3-4). Competitive tendering is being tried for the management of some prisons.

---

[1] For example, one health authority told the authors of the Report that in the case of hospital cleaning the contractor had been able to achieve labour productivity 40 per cent higher than the norm for the public sector, and 100 per cent higher than the previous average actual performance. This was done through better training, more and better supervision, better work practices, and a generally tougher régime.

In March 1992 the Treasury issued fresh guidance on 'market testing and buying in', reflecting changes called for in the November 1991 White Paper, *Competing for Quality*. The advantages of competitive tendering and potentially of buying in are described as including value for money, improved quality, innovation, the avoidance of uneconomical investment where technology is expensive and changing rapidly, flexibility where demand is erratic, and improved use of management resources. Few activities cannot (or should not) be subject to testing, and managers will be required to justify their decision not to market-test activities.[1] The final bid list should consist of not fewer than three nor more than six tenderers for a lump-sum contract, and not fewer than five nor more than eight for a reimbursable contract. Tenderers should be required to sign a confidentiality agreement to confirm that there has been no collusion with other contractors and no 'canvassing or soliciting' of government staff (MTBI, 1992, pp. 1-2, 4 & 13).

The period over which savings from contracting out should be assessed need not be tied to the duration of the contract. It is considered that, when comparing in-house and external bids, transfer costs such as redundancy payments should be spread over an appraising period of at least 10 years (MTBI, pp. 15 & 18). However, in a slightly earlier Treasury White Paper it is stated that

'We believe the right appraisal period will be not less than five and not more than ten years, depending on the commercial context and the degree of certainty on continuing cost and value for money savings' (CQBB, 1991, pp. 6-7).

The Local Government Act 1988 forbids councils to take various non-commercial considerations into account during the process of choosing contractors. In central government, however, the Treasury encourages some such considerations. It is recommended that potential contractors be asked to provide with their bid details such as the number and type of staff to be employed, including wage rates, bonus arrangements, conditions of employment and trade union representation (MTBI, p. 14). As Stephen Cirell and John Bennett point out, it is difficult to see why such matters should be relevant for a central government contract while irrelevant to a local

---

[1] Besides the terms 'contracting out' and 'buying in' (which appear to mean much the same), another term used is 'contracting in'—that is, bringing the contractor 'on site' to perform the task. To add to the confusion of descriptions, reference is also made to work being 'transferred out' (MTBI, 1992, pp. 6 & 17).

authority contract (*Local Government Chronicle*, 19 December 1991, p. 10).

The Ministry of Defence

The main department of central government to employ competitive tendering, apart from the Property Services Agency, is the Ministry of Defence (MoD), which is British industry's largest single customer. In this case it is the purchasing of equipment rather than of services which is mainly of interest. Nevertheless, there are very many examples of services which, in the jargon of the Ministry, have been 'contractorised'. They include such diverse activities as bird control, snow clearance, glass blowing, hairdressing, tailoring, medical services, laundry, lecturing, conservancy and scavenging (GCD, Annex S). Even advice on the preparation of contract specifications has itself been put out to tender (CQBB, p. 5).

Following the election of a Conservative government in 1979, Lord Rayner, as head of the Government's efficiency unit, studied the possibility of contracting out ancillary services. The motive was both to save costs and to reduce the number of civil servants. In the Ministry of Defence this involved a change to contract cleaning at some 850 establishments. As a result there was a reduction of over 6,000 full-time posts, standards were improved, and savings were over 40 per cent or almost £12 million a year (SITH, pp. 2-3).

In 1988 the MoD reported that it had made a major contribution to the Government's plans to reduce the size of the Civil Service. Since 1979 UK-based civilian staff numbers had decreased by over 100,000. Over 65 per cent of these savings had come about from a programme of efficiency measures, rationalisation of tasks, and contracting out (*Statement on the Defence Estimates 1988*, Vol. 1, p. 47). In 1989 it was stated that some 120 activities had been let to contract. The MoD seeks to ensure that defence support functions are carried out by the private sector unless it is more cost-effective, or operationally necessary, to keep the work in-house. This procedure is stated as having the following advantages: it improves efficiency and saves money without affecting standards of service; it allows Service manpower to be redeployed to front-line tasks; it encourages competition; and it frees departmental managers to concentrate on their essential business. Even where a task remains in-house, market testing produces savings of between 20 and 30 per cent (*Statement on the Defence Estimates 1989*, Vol. 1, p. 35).

In 1990 it was reported that application of competition to defence support services had, since 1979, produced net savings building up to some £55 million a year. Cleaning and catering contracts still constituted a large proportion of the savings, but more sophisticated activities such as air traffic control and engineering were being considered (*Statement on the Defence Estimates 1990*, Vol. 1, pp. 44 & 46). In 1992 the MoD stated that during 1990/91 its 'competition for services' programme, covering both military and civilian activities, accounted for 50 per cent of all central government department activity exposed to private-sector competition (*Statement on the Defence Estimates 1992*, p. 50).

A report early in 1991 by the Comptroller and Auditor General, John Bourn, head of the National Audit Office, examines the Ministry's initiatives in defence procurement (CAG). Over the previous five years the Ministry of Defence (referred to as 'the Department') spent over £40,000 million on equipment, stores and services. At the end of the 1970s much of the country's defence procurement was carried out by preferred contractors operating, in the case of development, on largely 'cost-plus' contracts. During the 1980s the Department adopted a more commercial approach, one of the main features of which was a drive to increase the proportion of contracts let competitively.

During the early 1980s the Department considered that it should be possible to raise the proportion of competitive contracts, and it estimated that savings of over 10 per cent might be realised. It sought also to define what it required in terms of key performance criteria, and to place with industry the responsibility for delivering equipment meeting those criteria. It now uses cost-plus contracts only where unavoidable. The proportion of work placed competitively (including that priced by reference to market forces) increased from 36 per cent in 1982-83 to 67 per cent by value in 1989-90. In the same period the proportion of 'cost-plus' contracts (based on actual cost plus a percentage fee) fell from 16 to 4 per cent by value.[1]

Examples of savings from the introduction of competition for the procurement of equipment are that of 10 per cent on four minehunters, of 40 per cent on a batch of respirators, and nearly 70 per cent on airframe fatigue testing. The Department told the House

---

[1] Other contracts are described as being either priced on estimates at the outset or as soon as possible thereafter, or based on 'cost incentive'—cost reimbursement with incentives to minimise costs. For the proportion of contracts which cannot be placed competitively, the Department have examined whether measures might be introduced that mimic some of the aspects of the competitive situation and thus give the contractors greater incentive to be more efficient. The greatest benefit would be had by having more contracts with a firm or fixed price from the outset, rather than by pricing taking place during the course of the work.

of Commons Defence Committee in 1988 that six projects valued at £2,000 million yielded savings of £250 million when put to competition. Further benefits of the commercial approach have included net savings of £350 million in 4½ years from the increased use of post-tender negotiation, and net savings of £250 million a year over the next 20 years when improvements in reliability and maintainability become fully effective.

The National Health Service

The National Health Service (NHS) is the largest employer in Europe. Initiatives to improve the efficiency of the domestic, catering and laundry support services (or 'hotel' services) began in 1980. As a result, in that year, and again in the following year, the then Minister of Health, Dr Gerard Vaughan, wrote to Regional Health Authorities, asking them to consider the possibility of contractual arrangements with the private sector. The response was unenthusiastic. Competitive tendering has been used for many years for the supply of goods, and for building and maintenance work; but the support services have generally been provided in-house without competition.[1]

Encouraging Competition

In September 1981 the new Health Minister, Norman Fowler, wrote to Regional Health Authorities demanding that they consider the use of contractors (Sheaff, 1988, p. 94). In September 1983 the Department of Health and Social Security (DHSS), and the corresponding departments in Scotland and Wales, issued circulars asking all health authorities to test the cost-effectiveness of the three 'hotel' services by use of competitive tendering, and asking them to develop the use of private contractors for other support services where savings could be made by doing so. Savings obtained would be available for patient care in the authority area concerned. Authorities were from 1 September 1983 to have refunded to them the value-added tax which they paid when using private contractors, but which did not apply to in-house work. The Fair Wages Resolution, which had applied to all public contracts and which required contractors to keep to wages and conditions of

---

[1] Spending on the support services by the NHS as a whole totalled £1,159 million in 1985-86, comprising £483 million for domestic services, £445 million for catering, and £231 million for laundry and linen services. In 1982-83 the proportion of NHS expenditure on ancillary services paid to contractors was 11·5 per cent for laundry services, 2·0 per cent for cleaning, and 0·2 per cent for catering, slightly less than in the previous four years (NAO, 1987, p. 6; Bach, 1990, p. 19).

employment established locally, was rescinded in September 1983. In its circular of September 1983, the DHSS recognised the importance of quality control, and in January 1986 it issued further guidance emphasising that monitoring is essential for services awarded both to private contractors and to in-house teams (NAO, 1987, pp. 6-7 & 22).

All district health authorities (DHAs) were asked to submit to regional health authorities (RHAs) timed programmes for implementation by the end of February 1984. A number of health authorities had not complied by then, and the DHSS was forced to change the date twice. In December 1983 the DHSS told authorities that, unless there were exceptional circumstances, all programmes were to be completed by September 1986. It is said that many authorities drew up timetables which were intended to delay and frustrate government instructions (NALGO, 1987, p. 11; NAO, 1987, p. 7). The three services affected by the competitive tendering policy directly employed in 1983 some 143,000 workers, about two-thirds of the ancillary workforce as a whole (Sheaff, 1988, p. 94). After re-election in 1987 the Government encouraged managers to contract out new activities but stopped short of making it mandatory to seek competitive tenders for portering and other services (Bach, 1990, pp. 20-21).

Perceived Drawbacks

According to a survey by the Association of Health Service Treasurers, analysed by Derek Harvey in 1981, most Health Authorities wished to continue to organise and manage directly-run services of their own.[1] The response of *Health and Social Services Journal* to the competition proposals made in the DHSS draft circular of February 1983 was:

---

[1] Domestic managers claimed four main drawbacks to contracting-out (Griffith, 1987, p. 162):

○ A very rigid service is provided, restricted to a literal interpretation of the contract. This often leads to staff disputes of a 'demarcation' type;

○ selection of a contractor could be 'hit and miss', and it is difficult to get rid of an unsatisfactory contractor quickly;

○ there were constant disagreements on standards of service with contractors reluctant to erode profit margins by eliminating any low standard of work brought to their attention;

○ the service provided by a contractor was as good as the local manager, and where there was a good manager he tended to move on quickly.

It would be wrong to claim that these problems cannot occur, but they do not prevent economical use being made of contractors in the business world generally. There are ways of dealing with these problems, which it is clearly one of the tasks of management in client organisations to learn.

'[A] blind prejudice against the health unions and a somewhat ill-defined desire to increase managerial efficiency are the motivating forces behind this piece of lunacy' (Griffith, 1987, p. 162).

Whether the *Journal*, and a number of Health Authorities, were themselves guilty of blind prejudice in their opposition to competition is perhaps indicated by the results, which are described below.

Tax Anomaly

There is an anomaly with regard to value-added tax (VAT) which in November 1991 the Government announced its intention to remove. This is that the NHS (and central government departments) paid VAT on services contracted out but not on those provided in-house. They could then obtain VAT refunds but only where the tax made the contracted-out service more expensive than in-house provision. If the external bid (including VAT) was cheaper, there was no refund. This created a perverse incentive to accept the lowest tender qualifying for a refund, rather than the one offering the best value. Therefore all new contracted-out services are eligible for refunds since November 1991, and all existing services will be eligible from April 1993. (The same applies to central government departments; local authorities are not affected since they are exempt from VAT.) (HM Treasury Press Release 62/91; CQBB, 1991, pp. 5-6.)

The Results of Competitive Tendering in the NHS

In the UK as a whole it is estimated by the Government that the drive to test NHS support services in the market has brought savings of over £626 million over seven years. Between 1984/85 and 1989/90 the cost of cleaning and other domestic services fell by 29 per cent in real terms (CQBB, 1991, pp. 14 & 17).

In a survey by Keith Hartley and Meg Huby in 1985, cases examined were those where the level of service which firms were contracted to provide was the same as that previously supplied in-house. The evidence from local authorities and the NHS suggested yearly savings from competitive tendering averaging 26 per cent, the range being from potential savings of 68 per cent to extra costs of 28 per cent. Interestingly, those health authorities without recent experience of contracting out were asked whether they expected the policy to result in cost savings. Out of 59 replies, 23 expected savings of 11 to 20 per cent, and 27 expected savings of 10 per cent or less (Hartley and Huby, 1985, p. 24).

National Audit Office Survey

In 1987 the National Audit Office (NAO) reported that, by the target date of 30 September 1986, health authorities had invited tenders for 68 per cent by value of the support services.[1] The need to draw up specifications adequate for tendering was found by the NAO to have caused authorities to undertake a thorough review of their service requirements. In comparing tenders, authorities were required to take into account the total estimated cost of redundancy and other severance costs. Of the contracts awarded, private contractors won 18 per cent. Divided by service, they won 24 per cent of contracts (32 per cent by value) in domestic services, 20 per cent (20 per cent by value) in laundry services and 4 per cent (7 per cent by value) in catering (NAO, pp. 3, 9 & 20). The low level of contracting out for catering reflects in part the dislike of the leading private caterers for the fixed-fee type of contracts, and for the prospect of working for unwilling clients (Bach, 1990, p. 24).

Annual cumulative savings as a result of tendering were estimated at £73 million, or 20 per cent of the previous cost of the services put to contract.[2] These savings are partly net of redundancy costs, etc. (expected to amount to £11·1 million by the end of 1986-87), but do not take into account the costs of tendering which the NAO estimated as broadly of the order of £15 million for the whole programme (largely a one-off cost). On the other hand, they exclude some savings generated before the end of 1984, as well as savings on contracts of £100,000 or less prior to June 1985, and they make no allowance for inflation occurring between the previous annual service cost and the contract price (NAO, pp. 12 & 15-16).

England

Over the years 1984 to 1989 inclusive, 1,515 contracts have been awarded by the NHS in England in the three areas subject to CCT.

---

[1] From a preliminary estimate of 1,652 contracts, it was found that 43 per cent of the total by value (by number 946 or 57 per cent) had been awarded, while invitations to tender had been issued for 25 per cent by value.

[2] Savings had been constant over the period of the initiative in laundry (about 14 per cent) and in catering (about 10 per cent). However, they had declined markedly for domestic services (from 32 to 18 per cent), and this was attributed by the DHSS to two factors: DHAs progressively reducing their costs prior to tendering, and some external tenders being very low in the early stages. Except for laundry, savings produced in-house were on average less than those obtained by contracting out. The average size of contracts (based on previous service costs) was £385,000. For domestic services and especially catering, those won by contractors were on average larger than those won in-house, but for laundry the averages were almost the same.

Table 10:
Growth of Contracting Out for Certain
NHS Services in England, 1986-90

Year ended 31 March	1986	1987	1988	1989	1990
			£ million		
Contract catering	2·9	7·5	10·7	12·9	16·1
Laundry contracts	7·8	9·4	11·5	12·4	12·7
Cleaning contracts	20·1	41·2	56·4	65·4	81·8
Patient care contracts	44·3	46·3	54·4	65·7	90·2

Source: HPSS (1991), pp. 27-29.

For domestic services 80 per cent of contracts were won in-house, for laundry services 83 per cent, and for catering 97 per cent; the overall proportion was 85 per cent. Annual savings in the first round totalled £110 million, of which 74 per cent were produced in-house. Domestic services produced savings of £82 million, catering over £18 million, and laundry over £9 million. In total, private contractors won 15 per cent of the contracts and produced 26 per cent of the savings. For subsequent rounds savings have not been monitored in the same detail but for the years 1989/90 and 1990/91 new annual savings are put at £5 million and £6 million respectively, so that total annual savings are now at least £121 million. Contracts are normally for a period of three years but may be extended to five years, particularly where substantial capital investment is involved (Department of Health, October 1991). The extent and growth of contracting for provision of certain services in the NHS in England are indicated by the figures given in Table 10 for revenue expenditure of Regional, District and Special Health Authorities. Although the figures are at current prices, by comparison expenditure for some other services, such as engineering maintenance and external building maintenance, has risen very little (HPSS, 1991, pp. 27-29).

Scotland

In Scotland health boards were advised in 1983 by the Scottish Home and Health Department to seek tenders, where there was sufficient capacity, for the same services as elsewhere, but the following year the three islands boards were exempted due to lack of interest by the trade. In 1984 each board and the Common Services Agency were required to complete a competitive tendering programme. However, five of the 15 boards, accounting for over half the relevant expenditure, declined to comply. The following year boards which decided not to proceed with tendering were given, as an interim measure, targets for savings to be achieved in-house. By the end of 1986 only 28 contracts, accounting for just 2 per cent of support services, had been awarded; four went to outside contractors. Only one of the health boards had submitted the long-term programme for competitive tendering requested in June 1984. For the 23 contracts (all but one of which were won in-house) for which figures were available at the end of 1986, savings were 14·5 per cent of previous service costs (NAO, pp. 24-26).

It was not until December 1987 that health boards in Scotland were effectively instructed to seek tenders. Nearly all contracts have been for a period of three years, though a few for laundry services have been for five years. On the 131 contracts awarded from then until the end of September 1991 (the majority of them in 1989), annual savings have been nearly £10 million for domestic services, over £6 million for catering, and over £1 million for laundry work. Aggregate savings as a proportion of pre-tender contract values were 18 per cent. Contracts won in-house were 82 per cent of the total, and they produced 72 per cent of the savings (Scottish Office, November 1991).

Wales

In Wales guidance on competitive tendering was given by the Welsh Office to the nine district health authorities and the Common Services Authority. As in Scotland, there was strong opposition from trade unions. In February 1985 the Welsh Office again requested programmes of action, and allowed two years for these to be put into effect. By September 1986 only 25 contracts, accounting for about 8 per cent of the total cost of support services, had been awarded; three went to outside contractors. Savings were on average 21·5 per cent of previous service costs (NAO, 1987, pp. 28-29). In August 1987 health authorities were required to test by competitive tendering at least 75 per cent of their domestic cleaning, catering and laundry services by December 1988. By the end of June 1989 savings on approximately 115 contracts were over £4 million (Welsh Office, December 1991).

CCT Attacked and Assessed

The policy of competitive tendering was not welcomed on all sides. The two unions organising the majority of ancillary staff (COHSE and NUPE) adopted policies in 1983 committing them to resist the government measure. Both unions encouraged local branches to persuade their own Authorities to refuse to implement competitive tendering, and this policy was also adopted by the TUC (Sheaff, 1988, p. 97).

Contracting out in the NHS was attacked by Rosie Newbigging and John Lister in a report in 1988 for London Health Emergency and the Association of London Authorities. They alleged:

'An ever-growing list of scandals and failures; a toll of suffering, inconvenience, hygiene risks and increased unpaid work foisted onto nursing and other NHS staff.' (Newbigging and Lister, 1988, p. 6)

Of over 1,000 contracts awarded, some 21 per cent were won by private firms, but in London, out of 132 contracts awarded, 45 per cent were won by private firms. Private contractors' main successes were relatively early in the tendering process. Tendering saved less than 10 per cent of the annual bill for catering, laundry and domestic services. Thousands of jobs have been lost, and the result was 'a massive reduction in hygiene and standards of care for patients' (Newbigging and Lister, 1988, pp. 6 & 8-9).

Management Reactions and Consequences

One author has suggested that competitive tendering in the NHS has not been a direct consequence solely, or even mainly, of government policy to require it. Although a few authorities were unco-operative, Mike Sheaff claims that this was on pragmatic grounds, with an almost universal desire being expressed to seek alternative means of achieving savings. He suggests that health authorities, while rejecting enforced contracting-out, generally welcomed competitive tendering as a way of making financial savings. One of the most significant results of tendering, Sheaff suggests, appears to have been a tightening of managerial control over employment, together with a shift towards greater local bargaining. Competitive tendering provided the opportunity to introduce, often with staff acquiescence, changes which managers already desired to make. These changes, rather than the introduction of 'market forces', represent in Sheaff's view the major impact of competitive tendering (Sheaff, 1988, pp. 93-95, 102 & 104).

Stephen Bach observes that

'A number of hospitals, particularly in London and the South East, which have a tradition of contracting out ancillary services, were originally motivated by their inability to recruit support staff on meagre NHS wage levels and turned to private provision.' (Bach, 1990, p. 17)

The most widespread use of private provision is for nursing staff.

Bach concedes that management can be attracted by the increased flexibility that contracting out can provide.[1] He states, however, that the term 'flexibility' is also used as a euphemism for desired changes in work organisation and implicitly as a way to reduce trade-union influence over working practices (Bach, 1990, pp. 17-18).

Contractors' Experiences

The experience of catering contractors in the NHS market has not been a happy one, according to the Treasury report in 1986, with the cost-effectiveness of staying in the market being an issue. They point out that catering tenders can cost up to £2,000 each to put together. With a 'success' rate at the time of about 1 in 15 bids, some £30,000 must be 'carried' on each contract, and this is not commercially feasible, particularly under a management-fee arrangement. Experience with the NHS had also led laundry contractors to mistrust tendering for public work, as they felt that costings were biased in favour of in-house operations, and that specifications were over-detailed and not always accurate (HMT, 1986, pp. 40-41). The sales and marketing director of one company admitted:

> 'Some contracts resulted in the companies concerned suffering significant losses. The main cause for this was their significant lack of experience in providing services for this particular market' (PE, 1990, p. 7).

According to the Joint NHS Privatisation Research Unit, contractors were initially very successful in terms of winning business. By March 1984 they were winning 74 per cent of contracts (90 per cent of domestic contracts), but this success did not last. A year later their share was just over half, and by December 1989 they had won only 23 per cent, that is, 439 out of a total of 1,910 contracts in the period 1983-89. Contractors won 27 per cent of cleaning, 26 per cent of laundry and 4 per cent of catering contracts. There is considerable regional variation, with the proportion of contracting out for laundry varying from none in Mersey and in Northern Ireland to 75 per cent in Oxford. The Unit (which is sponsored by a group of trade unions) adds that 'The organised opposition of health workers locally to the contractors

---

[1] Bach echoes here the thinking of Mike Sheaff:

'The real significance of competitive tendering has not been to prove the efficacy of market forces and competition. Instead, the manner in which management has used competitive tendering to increase their [sic] control over the labour process and to intensify work has been its major impact.' (Bach, 1990, p. 30)

has been effective in many cases in keeping them out, and also in discouraging them from even tendering'. Two groups of companies have between them 66 per cent of the cleaning contracts, three companies have 74 per cent of laundry contracts, and three other companies have 81 per cent of catering contracts; the proportions by value are said to be higher (PE, 1990, pp. 6-8).

Failures and Costs

The Unit states also that, out of 439 contracts awarded to companies, there have been 103 recorded failures, and that the rate of failure has increased. By 'failures' they mean cases where contractors have been sacked or have pulled out of contracts, or where there have been serious and substantiated complaints about their performance. However, they do acknowledge that 'Poorly thought out specifications have been a problem'. They see the programme of competitive tendering as carrying very substantial costs which fall into three broad categories: the costs of declining standards; the costs of driving down pay and making NHS workers unemployed; and the costs of arranging and evaluating bids and monitoring contracts.[1] The government, they say, has failed to monitor these costs (PE, 1990, pp. 4, 19 & 32-33; PAC, 1990, p. 4).

The allegation of widespread failure has been rebutted by the Contract Cleaning and Maintenance Association (since renamed the Cleaning and Support Services Association); they claim that many of the accusations are untrue, and that even the alleged failures listed were mainly over four years old. Nevertheless they state:

'We concede readily that there were some failures in the early days. . . . There were teething problems and mistakes on both sides. But the overwhelming evidence is that these initial problems are more than balanced by the gains that have been won.' (CCMA, 1990, p. 2)

They quote DHSS figures showing that the first round of tendering saved over £110 million, with private contractors saving the health service £32 million, while the remainder has been saved by health service staff responding to the competitive pressure from outside contractors (CCMA, 1990, pp. 2-3).

Bogus Savings?

According to Ben Griffith, Steve Iliffe and Geof Rayner in 1987: 'The "inefficiency" attributed to public services often refers to the

---

[1] The Unit has also criticised contracting out of portering and the record of contractors in this connection (PP, 1988).

perceived potential for increasing the exploitation of working people.' In their study of CCT in the NHS, they claim that the 'savings' achieved, while running into millions of pounds, are bogus:

'Counterbalancing any gains have been the losses through redundancy payments, administrative burden, lower morale, industrial action, increased exploitation and unemployment and, for some Districts at least, lower standards.' (Griffith, 1987, pp. 168-69)

On the other hand, they state that the available evidence does not allow them to conclude whether competition has resulted in genuine gains in efficiency,[1] and that it is impossible to say whether there has been significant 'over-manning' in the NHS domestic departments (Griffith, 1987, pp. 153, 166-70 & 172).

Learning from Experience

A detailed study of hospital cleaning by Simon Domberger, Shirley Meadowcroft and David Thompson in 1987 (Domberger, 1987) shows that, where tenders have been awarded to private contractors, costs are 34 per cent lower compared with cases where services have not been competed for. In the case of tenders awarded in-house on a competitive basis, the costs are 22 per cent lower. The difference between the costs at which private contractors and in-house units were operating appears to have been due at least in part to quality differences which in turn were partly due to inadequacies in specifications and in monitoring. Some of the contracts have gone wrong, with some contractors dropping out or seeking re-negotiation of contracts. When specifications are unclear, different bidders have to make their own assessments of what is required, and there is then the risk that the lowest bidder will be one who has underestimated the task. However, further analysis reveals that the situation developed and improved as contractors and clients got to know each others' needs better. The earlier contracts (those started before March 1984) were producing cost savings of 44 per cent, while later ones (awarded after March 1984) showed cost savings of 27 per cent. In addition, the incidence of contract failure declined steeply. This suggests that unrealistic bids were being made and accepted in the initial period, but that people were learning from experience and adjusting accordingly (TT, 1990, pp. 29-31).

---

[1] The authors rightly imply that it is by no means obvious that most waste or inefficiency was to be found in the 'ancillary' services. They point out, for example, that during the 1970s nursing staff in the NHS increased by 54 per cent, medical staff by 63 per cent, professional staff by 82 per cent, administrative staff by 103 per cent, and ancillary staff by 2·6 per cent.

Robin G. Milne has analysed six of the first contracts put out to tender in one (unnamed) regional health authority. In several cases only part of the hospital service was put out to contract, for two reasons: to test the competence and commitment of outside contractors, and to limit the damage from firms found lacking. However, contracts of short duration and covering only part of the service discouraged submissions. Average savings on the six contracts were 44 per cent, though much of this figure was due to reductions in the specifications of half the contracts. The introduction of competitive tendering was used by management as a device to alter services that were thought to have long needed changing. Milne notes the concern of district managements that poorly paid staff give poor-quality service, which no amount of monitoring will control satisfactorily; in such cases, going for the cheaper tender may well represent a false economy[1] (Milne, 1987, pp. 149, 151 & 153-54).

At the Bethlem Royal and Maudsley Hospitals five services— catering, laundry, domestic cleaning, and (in part) transport and gardening—have been contracted out for the best part of a quarter of a century. One of the reasons appears to have been difficulty in recruiting some categories of staff on the terms offered by the NHS. Although there have been financial savings and improvements in the services as a result of contracting out, one of the main benefits has been the freedom of manoeuvre and flexibility that contracting has produced (Paine, 1984, pp. 51-52).

According to the Cleaning and Support Services Association, during 1990 their members won 44 contracts from in-house organisations whilst six contracts were lost to in-house provision. In the first half of 1991 a further nine contracts were won by the membership whilst none was lost. At the end of June 1991 members were working in 295 hospitals—an increase of 94 over 18 months (SITH, pp. 7-8).

Scope for Extending Competition

The overall success of competitive tendering, despite a number of problems particularly in the initial stages, is such that it is now

---

[1] This observation fits in well with a comment made by Mike Davis, chairman of the Health Care Services Section of the Contract Cleaning and Maintenance Association:

'We wish to compete against in-house domestic service departments on terms of efficiency and productivity—not at the expense of lower staff wage rates. To underpay is detrimental to achieving good productivity and will, we believe, ultimately reduce standards' (Griffith, 1987, pp. 155-56).

widely accepted even by many who were initially sceptical or even hostile. Its extension would be beneficial, but there is still much inertia and resistance to be overcome.

Besides domestic services, laundry and catering, other services which have been suggested as suitable for competitive tendering— and in some cases have been put to tender by a few authorities— include portering, security, messenger work, ground maintenance, ambulance services, transport, medical records, computing, design, public relations, legal services, secretarial and clerical work, auditing, pharmacy and laboratory work, and pathology. Although a large proportion of legal requirements is bought in, relationships with particular firms are frequently long-standing and not regularly reviewed. Such cosy arrangements should not continue unquestioned (Robertson, 1992, p. 55).

Hospitals account for more than 60 per cent of the cost of the NHS, so competitive tendering for their management could have a far greater impact than the comparatively marginal one produced by tendering for ancillary services. The potential for greater efficiency in the management of many hospitals is almost certainly large, and thus also the possible improvements in both patient care and costs. Competitive tendering for hospital management has been used successfully in the United States and in Canada[1] (Davis, 1985, pp. 5 & 20-24).

It is neither necessary nor practical to introduce tendering for management into all of more than 2,000 hospitals at once, but the idea does need to be tested. A modest and cautious trial has been proposed by Dave Davis. A few hospitals—enough to allow useful comparisons (perhaps a dozen or so)—should be carefully chosen, and tenders invited for their management. The patient care specified should be at least as good as that currently provided, and Davis suggests three levels of protection for patients so as to ensure their good treatment in all events, and to reassure those in doubt about the experiment. A small trial of this nature could be of enormous advantage. The risks are small, whilst the benefits are likely to be large (Davis, 1985, pp. 29-33).

---

[1] For example, a poorly managed hospital in Hawkesbury, Ontario, was transformed by contracting-out of its management at the beginning of 1983. Both staff morale and patient care improved, as better methods and services were introduced. Department heads were given responsibility and resources, and specialist advice was made available. In addition to all this, in the first year under new management a substantial deficit was turned into a large surplus.

SIX

Experience Abroad

This chapter discusses the experience of, and attitudes towards, competitive tendering and contracting-out elsewhere in the world. Reports from Australia, Europe, Japan, Canada and the United States are examined in turn, and favourable results are found in very many instances. In the case of the United States we look at the tax revolt and experience there of private police and of fire, medical, social and other services, as well as some of the evidence in public transport and education.

An International Survey

In a survey in 1990 of council services in France, Denmark, Canada and the USA, David Green states:

'In all the countries and practically all the towns and cities visited "competition" was a live and emotive subject. Nowhere, however, was it yet being enforced by central government as it is here, save in respect of those instances where funds were being provided by central government or "State" for use at County or City level on behalf of the others. The movement towards increasing the level of competition was largely fired by the local authorities themselves. . . . Thus, the traditional and almost total reliance by British local authorities on direct labour for the provision of these services is clearly exceptional. In France the use of contractors is fairly widespread and has been for as long as can be remembered. Likewise in Denmark and America. . . . The main comparator in determining who should do what was cost—service levels being pre-set in the contract documents. . . . But the real difference between competition here and elsewhere is its imposition in Britain by Central Government on Local Government via a legalistic framework. Even in France where much of local government is controlled from the centre . . ., there was no hint of such an approach on the horizon. Competition began and ended with the authorities themselves' (Green, 1990, sections 8.1-8.6).

However, in his summary of conclusions Green writes:

'Local Government in Britain enjoys a high degree of autonomy but fails to use it as constructively as it might. . . . There is far higher dependence on in-house delivery of public services in Britain than in any of the other countries visited . . . and historically that has probably inhibited initiative and change. All countries visited were either already well committed to competition of these activities or well advanced in opening more up to competition . . . The greater the dependence on raising funds locally with their use/application open to public scrutiny and criticism, the greater the likely interest in local government and value for money and quality. . . . We are behind the USA and Canada in performance monitoring—particularly on quality and customer satisfaction—and it shows' (Green, 1990, section 17.1).

The heavy dependence of local government in Britain on funds from central government is likely to be one reason for the lack of interest locally in (voluntary) competitive tendering. Local government is not immune from the effects of dependency and the attitudes it fosters.

Australia

New South Wales has saved A$75 million in two years by tendering out areas such as catering, cleaning and laundry in hospitals. Professor Domberger of Sydney University has estimated that A$2,500 million could be saved in Australia by tendering out services such as cleaning, laundry, computer services, catering, maintenance and construction. Many councils make extensive use of contracting, and the federal government has moved towards increased contracting (Shann, 1990).

Simon Domberger and David Henscher surveyed 238 government departments, authorities and councils in respect of their experience with cleaning and waste collection contracts. One finding was that the likelihood of deterioration in a contractor's performance is positively related to the frequency of selection of the cheapest tender. Contractors with good credit ratings seem to provide the best service, and the best-performing contracts appear to be those where bids are invited only from tenderers which fulfil certain advertised criteria. It is suggested that incentives, such as the carrot of contract renewal, are more important than financial penalties in improving contract performance.[1]

Europe

In a detailed survey of competitive tendering in the European Community, Lee Digings also states that the UK is the exception in making competitive tendering obligatory. In the other countries of the Community, in the majority of cases contracts tend to be let to private contractors for purely pragmatic reasons with no ideological undertones; although there are exceptions, it generally remains a fundamentally unpoliticised issue (Digings, 1991, p. 16).

---

[1] Michael Stutchbury, 'Inside the black box of contracting out', *The Australian Financial Review*, 19 October 1990, p. 71.

In Denmark it is estimated that about 15 per cent of all public-sector cleaning is contracted out. There is an interesting arrangement in Arhus, the second largest Danish city, where domestic refuse collection is carried out by a non-profit society which has a 25-year concession from the council. In France, local authorities have frequently chosen to involve the private sector[1] in the provision of services (Digings, 1991, pp. 58-59). Digings observes that

> 'Authorities of all political complexions from the Gaullist RPR to the Communist PCF have put their cleansing operations into private hands with the result that some 60 per cent of domestic refuse collection is now in the private sector'. (ALA, p. 6)

In Paris the authorities regard the cleaning contractors as dependable allies, and Digings notes that their methods do produce results, such that Paris is now a far cleaner city than it used to be (ALA, p. 6). In Germany it is estimated that at least half or thereabouts of the refuse collection, about a fifth of street cleaning, about 60 per cent of ground maintenance, and about 90 per cent of window cleaning are contracted out.

Italy has one of the most extensive systems of municipal enterprise, but has also witnessed some sweeping attempts at privatisation which have invariably been linked with political intrigue and scandals.[2] In the Netherlands contracting out of local services is widespread. Over 40 per cent of the municipalities have contracted out building cleaning, almost half have 'privatised' ground maintenance, and more than a third the management of sport centres. Refuse collection and street cleaning are often contracted out by the smaller Dutch municipalities. According to a Dutch report, the average hourly rates of municipal parks departments are 43 per cent higher than in the private sector and productivity is 19 per cent lower. In Spain most construction work is contracted out, as are often services such as refuse collection and street cleaning (Digings, pp. 49-50, 73-74, 85, 107, 121-122 & 141).

In Denmark a company in the private sector, Falcks Redningskorps, provides almost half the fire protection and nearly

---

[1] Contracting out by the larger towns was less common until recently when Paris adopted a programme of 'privatisation'. Ground maintenance is mainly in municipal hands, apparently largely because wage rates are as high, if not higher, in the private sector than in the public sector.

[2] The labyrinthine procedures for public contracts in Italy are subject to hundreds of laws as well as, it is said, to a system of 'favours' and not infrequently organised crime.

all of the ambulance service. The fire services are provided under contract to about two-thirds of the local authorities, and must meet closely defined national standards. In a study in 1983, Ole Kristensen analysed the costs of fire protection in 241 Danish municipalities. He found that public provision cost nearly three times as much as private provision. This difference was only partly explained by two factors: private provision is more frequent in less urbanised municipalities; and urbanisation increases costs somewhat. Falck was found to be more innovative than public fire departments, and to have been responsible for a number of improvements in fire-fighting technology (Kristensen, 1983, pp. 4-5 & 7-8; Simmonds, 1989, pp. 30-32).

Japan

In comparison with Britain, Japan has fewer than half the local government personnel per head, and only one-third as many civil servants (Ivens, 1992, p. 6). Contracting out by local authorities in Japan developed in the 1950s as a response to the financial deficits many of them experienced. It was recommended in 1966 by a Local Government Research Council for such areas as refuse collection, management of day nurseries, school catering and cleaning, and the maintenance of town halls. As a result the Ministry of Home Affairs encouraged or pushed local authorities to use private contractors (Itani, 1989, p. 52).

Extensive and increasing use has been made of contracting out. A survey by the Ministry of Home Affairs in 1980 showed that, excluding construction which was not covered by the survey, 47 services and 669 local authorities were involved. Allowing for the fact that not all services were provided by all towns, the overall rate of contracting out was found to be 46·6 per cent. The proportion of individual services contracted out varied from almost nil to nearly 85 per cent, the highest rates being for some cleaning services, night security services and certain specialised activities such as microfilming, and the surveying and mapping of roads. Most of the contractors—nearly 70 per cent—were private companies, but 18 per cent were individuals who were used mainly on a local basis, for example for reading of water meters. Other types of contractors (together under 14 per cent) included regional associations of local governments and residents' associations. The most popular method of choosing a contractor was by negotiation. Invited bidding was dominant in only two areas: designing public facilities and surveying roads. Competitive tendering was not generally used, although it was being encouraged by the Ministry of Home Affairs as the fairest to bidders and the most favourable to the municipality. The Ministry surmised that the reason for the predominance of negotiated contracts was the large number of relatively small contractual jobs (Marlin, 1982, pp. 5-9).

The intended benefits of contracting-out were seen as improving efficiency, getting the use of specialist skills, cutting costs, reducing staff levels, improving the quality of services, and allowing public participation. Reducing staff levels was seen as less important than cutting costs, while public participation was a significant reason in only two services. Use of outside contractors was considered to be very successful: efficiency was thought to be increased in 80 per cent of cases, costs were down in 51 per cent, the service was improved in 57 per cent, and the staff level was down in 66 per cent (but up in 9 per cent). Many towns claimed a cost reduction of over 30 per cent from contracting out refuse collection, in addition to an improvement in service quality (Marlin, 1982, pp. 13-15).

Despite legal problems which have restricted its growth in some activities, contracting out is firmly established and widely used in Japan. Of 674 towns (including special wards), the cleaning of the town hall has been contracted out in almost every one. Nearly all towns have contracted out one or more aspects of all or part of their activities (Itani, 1989, pp. 51-52 & 54).

Canada

Local governments accounted for 30 per cent of all government expenditure in Canada in 1983, and provided between them a wide range of services. In 1981-82 James McDavid conducted a survey of about 200 municipalities across Canada with populations of over 10,000. Replies were received from 136 municipal managers (McDavid, 1988). Of all contracts for which details were received, the most were for waste management (26·4 per cent) and construction and maintenance (26·4 per cent), followed by those for protection of persons and property—that is, police services, animal control and pest control (22·5 per cent). Smaller proportions were for administration (7·3 per cent), social and cultural services (6·8 per cent), transportation (6·5 per cent) and other services (3·9 per cent).

McDavid completed in 1981-82 a second survey specifically on residential solid-waste collection services. Questionnaires were sent to municipal engineers of towns with a population of more than 10,000 and subsequently, in cases where the service had been contracted out, to the private contractors concerned. Of the 200 municipalities questioned, replies were received from 126. Of these, 42·1 per cent had contracted out the service, 37·3 per cent had a mixture of private and municipal services, and 20·6 per cent used only their own employees.[1]

Analysis of the variation in costs took into account the following factors: total weight of waste collected, frequency of collection, location of collection, population density, and annual temperature variation. After adjustment for these factors, using only private contractors was found on average to cost 29 per cent less than using only in-house teams.[2]

Using a mixture of in-house labour and contracting-out seems to have several advantages, particularly for local authorities whose members and managers are cautious about making radical changes yet wish to learn directly from experience. Even if the result were eventually to be the contracting out of all provision of a particular service, a gradual approach allows time both for municipal employees to find alternative employment, and for the authority to gain experience of using private contractors. Clearly a much larger proportion of towns in Canada than in the UK show themselves willing to experiment and to learn.

McDavid reports that one small town, Metchosin in British Columbia, with a population of 3,500, 'operates with three full-time employees: a manager, a secretary and an accounting clerk. All its services are provided through contracts (public and private producers are both involved) and service agreements'.

The United States

For those interested in more efficient government services, a systems and operations research analyst in the United States, Robert W. Poole, Jr., offered advice on how local government can provide better services at lower cost in a 200-page book, *Cutting Back City Hall*. Many of the examples and comparisons which follow are taken from his book, which was published in 1980, and were therefore available to inquirers over a decade ago. Local authorities in Britain could have learned from them, had they been interested. However, the title of Poole's book might not have attracted their interest.

---

[1] However, those towns which contracted out none of the work included a higher proportion of the larger towns and thereby accounted for about 30 per cent of the total population served.

[2] Before applying these adjustments, the apparent saving was nearly 34 per cent. For towns using a mixture of public and private services the unadjusted savings, at 26 per cent, were still considerable.

The Tax Revolt

One of the most important reasons for the growth of contracting out in the United States was the so-called tax revolt. The biggest blow to the growing demands of local government for ever-increasing taxes was the decision by a two-to-one majority of voters in California to support 'Proposition 13'. This had the effect of reducing by 8 per cent total state and local taxation in California. Subsequently voters in many other states also reduced taxes or imposed spending limits. In 1979 a survey of 50 states found that in 37 of them taxes had been reduced or spending limits imposed (Poole, 1980, p. 17).

This reaction should be seen against a background of municipal revenue having increased in the country as a whole by over 186 per cent (against a general rise in prices of 70 per cent) over the nine-year period 1967-76—a compound average increase of over 12 per cent per year. Local government employees had risen in number by 114 per cent between 1960 and 1975, against an increase of 19 per cent in federal government employment. Professor J. K. Galbraith failed to discourage this growth when he said in 1975 that 'no problem associated with New York City could not be solved by providing more money'. New York City duly spent and spent, but was far from alone in this[1] (Poole, 1980, pp. 19-21). Finally, the taxpayers rebelled, and demanded moderation in the taking and spending of money that had been theirs.

Police

Even before the taxpayers' revolt there were scattered cases of private provision of what are normally considered government services. Since the 1850s there have been private police officers in San Francisco—trained, armed, and with full powers of arrest, but not paid for out of taxes. Poole describes a variety of ways in which police forces can be made more efficient, and concludes with this comment:

'The innovations discussed here are disarmingly simple. Yet most have been adopted in only a handful of police departments and only in the last five to ten years. Why? Unfortunately, police departments—like government agencies generally—are very resistant to change. . . . police departments all too frequently have continued to operate in the same manner, year after year, decade after decade' (Poole, 1980, p. 49).

---

[1] Poole comments: 'Fostering the arts, aiding the handicapped, employing the down-and-out, filling up people's leisure hours, demonstrating solar technology—you name it and some local government somewhere has done it.'

Fire Services

Fire protection is an example of government provision leading to a waste of resources since the provision of 'free' public services leads to overinvestment in fire suppression and underinvestment in fire prevention. Less money would need to be spent in total on fire protection if more property owners invested in protective measures (Poole, 1980, pp. 32-33 & 62). As to the method of providing fire-fighting services, privately organised services in the United States (where most firefighters are volunteers) are not only very widespread but also very varied; almost without exception they are less costly than conventional government fire departments. One of the leading private fire-fighting services, Rural/Metro Fire Department, charged customers, even if far from the nearest fire hydrant, less each year than a quarter of the equivalent national average cost for this service. A variety of innovations enabled the company to operate at such low cost (Poole, 1980, p. 66).

When the town of Scottsdale in Arizona was incorporated in 1952, instead of starting a municipal fire department, Rural/Metro was given a renewable contract to provide the service. In 1976 an evaluation of the service provided in this town of 90,000 people found that it was comparable with that in three similar nearby towns, but nearly 40 per cent cheaper than the least expensive of the other three towns' municipal fire services (Poole, 1980, p. 71).

Medical and Social Services

On emergency ambulance service, Poole states that

'A study by the Illinois Department of Transportation showed that private paramedic service costs, on average, about half that of the public service. The Ambulance Medical Service Association of America found the cost of private service to be one-third that of government service'[1] (Poole, 1980, p. 86).

Contracting out for social services was found by the Urban Institute to be 'fairly common' following amendments to the Social Security Act in 1967 and 1975, day care being the service most frequently involved. In one county, use of a private contractor for outpatient treatment of alcoholics produced savings of well over 50 per cent (Poole, 1980, pp. 127-28). Another trend which Poole found

---

[1] As an example, in 1975 Glendale in California abolished its paramedic unit and contracted with two ambulance firms to provide the three paramedic units it required, at an annual cost over 70 per cent less than that estimated for municipal provision; very satisfied with the service received, the town subsequently renewed the contract.

was for towns and hospital societies to contract out hospital management. The typical management contract costs a non-profit hospital from 3 to 8 per cent of its annual income, but the savings are generally three to five times as much as the cost of the contract (Poole, 1980, p. 132).

Other Services

Savings of about 20 per cent were obtained by several towns in California when contracting out ground or park maintenance[1] (Poole, 1980, pp. 105-106). Professional services are contracted out in some cases, specifically engineering services, legal services and, less often, planning services. The outputs of these services are often difficult to measure or specify in contracts, so value-for-money comparisons are difficult. Moreover, few of the contracts for professional services were found to be awarded on the basis of competitive tendering. However, an evaluation of property-tax assessment in different states found not only that the standard of assessment work was highest in Ohio, but also that the cost of assessment in Ohio, which contracts out this work, was only half the average for other states (Poole, 1980, pp. 163-64).

Public Transport

While only indirectly related to the subject of contracting out, public transport illustrates the potential inadequacies of a service which is heavily regulated and often provided by government. Public transport in most towns consists of a network of buses running on fixed routes, and some taxis which are usually restricted in number as well as in other ways. What is often really needed to supplement these two 'extremes' (buses and taxis) are other forms of transport which are more flexible than buses and available where needed, but much cheaper than taxis. One example of this is the 'jitney', a vehicle which typically carries between 8 and 12 passengers along a relatively fixed but customer-oriented route.[2]

---

[1] One town was amazed when contractors trimmed 500 trees in a week—as many as the 'city crew' had trimmed in a year. Another town was losing $60,000 a year on its golf course when it decided to contract out its management. The winning bidder signed a 30-year lease contract, rebuilt the course, and guaranteed the town a minimum income of $60,000 a year.

[2] Their potential variety is illustrated by Poole with examples from Pittsburgh where, despite being illegal, they flourished:

'Some parallel the bus lines, charging the same 40c fare, but for a little extra they will take a passenger home. Others drive what amount to car-pool routes, picking up the same passengers day after day and taking them to and from work. Some

[Cont'd. on p. 135]

Analysis by Roger Teal of contracting out for public transport services has shown that while transitional costs are sometimes significant, they delay rather than erode the savings available. Federal government law prohibits the laying off of public workers through privatisation of bus services, so that only natural loss or attrition and early retirement can be used to reduce staff numbers. Over a period, however, significant cost savings are achieved, particularly by the third year of a contract. Teal's analysis strongly indicates cost savings in the range of 22-39 per cent for fixed-route services, and over 50 per cent for demand-responsive service. Moreover, these savings were maintained over five years so they were apparently not the result of artificially low bids used to gain contracts. Teal found that cost savings appear to be more robust under competitive-bidding circumstances. The findings are less clear on the question of quality, with some studies showing marked improvements under private contracting, and others showing problems (PR, 1991, p. 17). It would appear that careful choice of contractor is an important element in the success of competitive tendering.

Refuse Collection

Refuse collection is another service which can benefit from better management and from innovation. When Professor E. S. Savas studied the costs of residential rubbish collection in New York, he found that the municipal service cost $297 a year in 1975 for collection twice a week in one area, whereas three miles away in a similar area just outside the city a private firm provided collection three times a week for $72 a year. Such findings led the Citizens Budget Commission to recommend changing to private contractors at a saving of over $60 million a year. In San Francisco in 1975, households paid about $40 a year for rubbish collection, and the city's Public Works Director was frank about the situation: 'I shudder to think what would happen if my department was responsible for collecting garbage ... the rates would go through the roof' (Poole, 1980, p. 89).

A very large study in 1975 and 1976 by Professors E. S. Savas and Barbara J. Stevens of Columbia University covered refuse

---

wait in front of supermarkets to take shoppers home. Occasionally drivers will extend credit to regular passengers until payday. Besides supplying convenient low-cost transportation to low-income people, jitneys also provide self-employment to the owner-drivers, with compensation in direct proportion to how hard they work. Jitneys are a perfect example of a form of transportation that fits the changing needs of its riders.' (Poole, 1980, p. 114)

collection in 1,378 communities with populations between 2,500 and 750,000. Four types of provision were distinguished:

(i)   municipal collection;

(ii) contract collection, where a single company is paid by the town;

(iii) franchise collection, where private contractors are each assigned an area of the town, and are paid by their customers;

(iv) private collection, where private firms compete for individual customers.

Contract and franchise services were found to be the least costly for towns of all sizes. However, for towns with a population of less than about 20,000 the differences were relatively small, whereas for those with populations of over 50,000 they were very large. Among the latter, the typical municipal service cost 68 per cent more than the average contractor to provide kerbside collection twice a week. The municipal organisations evidently lack the incentive to be efficient.[1] It was also found that municipal services tend to 'overproduce'; when given a choice, residents tend to prefer a less expensive refuse service even if this means a reduced level of service (Poole, 1980, pp. 89-91).

Middletown, Ohio, switched from municipal to contract service for refuse collection in 1972, saving $350,000 a year. Camden, New Jersey, did the same in 1974, and saved $700,000 a year. Quite a few large cities in the United States, and in Canada, divided up their territories into refuse collection districts, putting some or all of them out to bid. For example, Montreal kept 18 districts for municipal collection, while contracting out for 180 districts; the largest contractor serves 68 of these but some serve only one district each. This method not only facilitates comparisons but also allows both large and small contractors to obtain business—an example which could usefully be followed elsewhere. Similarly, St. Paul, Minnesota uses 40 to 50 companies, Minneapolis uses 50, and Wichita uses 80 (Poole, 1980, p. 92). This is in marked contrast to the often huge authority-wide contracts specified by the larger local authorities in Britain.

---

[1] Their employees are absent 12 per cent of the time against 7·5 per cent for the private contractors, they use much larger crews (on average 3·26 against 2·18), serve fewer households per shift (632 against 686), and spend more time per household per year (4·35 man-hours against 2·37).

Education

Education is one of the most expensive activities of government. In the United States the cost per pupil of publicly funded schools rose by 175 per cent in real terms between 1950 and 1976. Despite this, results did not improve but actually declined.[1] Some 40 per cent of employees (in some districts as many as 60 per cent) were not engaged in teaching, but teachers had increased in number and class sizes had decreased—without evident benefit. The average cost of publicly funded schooling in 20 cities in 1976 was $1,765 per pupil (against a national average of $1,740), with a range of $1,142 to $2,425. By comparison, private schools (attended by about 10·6 per cent of pupils) had a wider range of costs but included large numbers of schools at which cost per pupil was often less than $1,000, partly because of smaller administrative overheads. The average cost per pupil for the 9,822 Catholic schools was between $500 (elementary) and $1,036 (secondary), while that for the 2,200 Lutheran schools was $600 (Poole, 1980, pp. 173-75 & 184). Subject to more detailed evaluation, it would appear that there was, and probably still is, inefficiency in the management of publicly funded schools.

The Extent of Contracting Out

A survey of all but the smallest 'cities' and counties, sponsored in 1987 by Touche Ross, the International City/County Management Association (ICMA) and the Privatization Council, found that just over three-quarters of the respondents had recent experience of contracting out at least one service. Although only 19 per cent of recipients completed the survey questionnaire, respondents were found to contract out services estimated to total more than $1,000 million a year. The main reason for contracting out, though not the only one, was to save costs. Of those that sought savings, 40 per cent saved at least 20 per cent, and 10 per cent of them saved 40 per cent or more. At least a fifth of respondents had neither used contracting out in the previous five years, nor planned to use it in the next two years; their most frequently given reason was a belief that that there would be no savings or other benefits. Other reasons given included lack of control, trade union or employee resistance, and lack of interest by the private sector (particularly in rural areas). Impediments to contracting out also included politics, bureaucratic

---

[1] The proportion of those who were 'functionally illiterate' rose over a decade from 11 to 16 per cent, while scores on standardised tests of reading, writing and mathematical ability declined significantly after the mid-1960s.

inertia, lack of awareness, and public opinion. Bureaucratic inertia appeared to be a more significant impediment for larger governments.

Services most frequently contracted out were solid-waste collection or disposal (nearly 60 per cent of respondents), vehicle towing or storage (45 per cent), building or grounds maintenance and service (nearly 45 per cent), administration (36 per cent), traffic-signal or street-lighting services (32 per cent), and data processing (31 per cent). In most cases the lowest bids are selected; but in many cases governments select what is described as the most responsive bidder—which may not always be the lowest. It is not uncommon for the chosen contractor to be another government, nor for a contract to be for only a portion of a service (such as for part of the geographical area) (David, 1988, pp. 43-45, 47 & 53).

According to an estimate in 1986, state and local governments were thought to contract out the supply of services to the extent of some $100,000 million a year (Martin, 1992, pp. 12 & 15). Research in 1990 by The Mercer Group of management consultants showed that 74 per cent of towns and 83 per cent of counties surveyed thought privatisation would increase, while only 5 per cent thought it would decrease. Moreover, 69 per cent of the towns and 67 per cent of the counties indicated that they plan to privatise in the future. All respondents claimed to have achieved financial savings through contracting out, and 45 per cent claimed that improved quality of work was a significant benefit. Surprisingly, over half of the contracts reviewed are for only one year. Contract sizes varied widely, from tens of thousands to millions of dollars a year, the largest being for major construction projects and transit system management. Most contracts are awarded as a result of competitive bidding. Key factors influencing the choice of a contractor were thought by 59 per cent to include potential service quality, and by 40 per cent to include financial considerations—not just cost but also financial stability and willingness to put up bonds (PR, 1991, pp. 11-13).

Employment and Management

In a survey by the National Commission on Employment Policy in 1989 on the long-term employment implications of privatisation, the consequences for 34 town and county services privatised over the previous 10 years were reviewed. Of the 2,213 public employees concerned, after privatisation 54 per cent were hired by the private contractors, 24 per cent were found other government positions, 7 per cent retired and 7 per cent were laid off. Workers' wages were not significantly reduced in most cases, though employee benefits were often less for private-contractor employees. Labour turnover of private contractors, a key indicator of job satisfaction, compared favourably with the national average. The main means used by private contractors to cut costs appeared to be reductions in overheads, use of better equipment, and higher worker productivity; mentioned a little less often by contractors were lower pay/benefits for workers and more efficient management. Savings from privatisation were used in a third of cases examined to expand other services, and in a further quarter of cases to expand the service in question (PR, 1991, pp. 11-12 & 15).

Further Evidence

Services which have been 'privatised' (contracted out) in the United States include a wide variety. For example, Madeira County in California claims to be saving $250,000 a year through private-sector provision of lawyers, while Orange County in the same state has instituted a policy of requiring defence lawyers to offer bids for their services before they can be appointed to represent indigent murder defendants; this system apparently saved the county $400,000 on one trial alone.

Contracting-out of services provided by the federal government has been encouraged by both Republican and Democratic administrations. Most federal agencies, other than the Department of Defense (which employs contracting-out on a very large scale), have been required since 1976 to make comprehensive studies of their activities. A service must be contracted out if a private contractor is 10 per cent cheaper, a figure which is presumably meant to allow for a margin of error and for monitoring costs. However, the requirement for cost studies is followed spasmodically, and departments vary considerably in their enthusiasm for cost comparisons.

One advantage enjoyed by private organisations is that their employees can be rewarded more quickly for good performance, which is good for morale. On the other hand, rules in the civil service often penalise better employees. However, one US survey found that a key reason for abandoning the option of contracting out was employee and union resistance (Rehfuss, 1989, pp. 13, 15-18, 23, 49 & 58).

A study by the US Department of Housing and Urban Development in 1984 found that many services provided by municipalities were more expensive than the same service provided privately, by a margin ranging from 28 to 96 per cent (Seader, 1986, p. 9). The widespread and increasing use of competitive tendering and contracting out in the United States reflects their value in both improving services and reducing costs.

SEVEN

Conclusions and Recommendations

Conclusions

Central government, local government and the National Health Service employ millions of people in the United Kingdom and spend many thousands of millions of pounds every year. The money they spend is obtained overwhelmingly not from charges or fees but from taxes. The efficiency or otherwise of these bodies is of considerable importance for the welfare of the whole population. Competitive tendering has much to offer in this respect, although like any tool or technique it needs to be used well to obtain the best results: it is clear from the evidence reviewed that neither competitive tendering nor contracting-out is an automatic route to success and that both have their pitfalls.

Successful use of competitive tendering depends on carefully thought out specifications for the services involved as well as good monitoring of the chosen contractors' work and prompt action to deal with any problems which arise. Success is unlikely to come from simply appointing a contractor, whether internal or external, and then forgetting the matter until it is time to invite tenders again.

Improvements in Efficiency and Quality

The evidence from the Audit Commission and others is clear and abundant that competitive tendering can, and in many areas usually does, produce significant improvements. It frequently saves money, whether or not the work is won in-house or by an outside contractor. Moreover, thanks to the introduction, very often for the first time, of clear specifications and of service monitoring, quality is usually either maintained or improved. The beneficial results have progressively overwhelmed the difficulties and sometimes the failures which have also accompanied its use, particularly in the early experimental stages. While direct labour is not always or inevitably inefficient, there is a strong tendency for it to be so in the absence of competition. The policy of direct employment, coupled with dependence on taxation and absence of competition, leads to inefficiency and thus deprives taxpayers and the public in general of value for money. The argument holds good not only for local authorities but also for other institutions, in particular for central government and the National Health Service.

Contracting Out and Competitive Tendering

Contracting out appears from the evidence often to lead to greater savings than can be achieved by improving in-house efficiency. More important, however, is competitive tendering. Whatever the outcome, it is competition which encourages efficiency and which is a more important factor than the ownership of the successful contractor. In practical terms it is therefore sufficient to ensure fair and free competition, and to let it determine where the greatest efficiency is to be obtained in any particular instance.

Indifference and Hostility to Competitive Tendering

Many sections of government have been slow to realise, or apparently even to think about, the benefits they might obtain in this way, despite the evidence which has long been available. In addition to their lack of enterprise in this matter—itself an indication of the inefficiency of monopoly provision of services— there has been much active opposition to competition within government circles.

Bureaucracy, socialism and conservatism have all contributed elements of opposition to the introduction of competitive tendering. Many local authorities in particular are still hostile towards any possibility of contracting out, while the public-sector unions remain the most vigorous opponents of competition. However, even the more moderate councils generally failed, prior to legislation, to test the efficiency of their in-house works and service departments by obtaining quotations from the private sector. This widespread reluctance either to find out the facts about their in-house operations, or to do anything effective about them, was all the more noteworthy in organisations whose proclaimed aim is not private profit but public service.

The need for compulsion has its disadvantages. It inevitably introduces rules, some of which are bound to be restrictive, as well as causing additional work and antagonism. However, central government supplies most of the money spent by local authorities, and nearly all of that spent by health authorities; so it has to take an interest in minimising the waste of these resources. Whether local councils would prefer greater independence at the price of reducing their income from central government grants is a matter for them to ponder. Meanwhile, the policy of compulsory competitive tendering has been vindicated by the inefficiency it has exposed and the results it has achieved.

Management and Organisation

As some health and local authorities now admit, the introduction of competition has had a considerable beneficial effect on their management and organisation. Aspects of good management which had often been badly neglected, such as the monitoring of services, are at last starting to receive the attention they deserve. The separation of client and contractor roles is an important development which leads in turn to better attitudes towards those whom these organisations are meant to serve. Some authorities are even slowly beginning to realise that they exist to serve not themselves and their employees but the public, even though they would deny that they ever thought otherwise. DSOs are becoming better organised, and the public are starting to get the benefit of more efficient services, however provided.

Obstacles to Competitive Tendering

There is much suspicion, and some evidence, that many authorities are still obstructing fair competition. Private contractors are often reluctant to tender for the provision of government services so long as they find that the time and money spent in submitting tenders is rarely successful, and while they fear that even if work is obtained the client will be unwilling and resentful. Partly as a result, in some areas of the country competition is more theoretical than real, although the mere possibility of competition has had the beneficial effect of waking-up some sleepy DSOs and improving their efficiency.

Scope for Competitive Tendering

Activities of local authorities for which competitive tendering has been suggested or practised include architectural services, legal services, careers advice, accountancy, personnel, residential care, 'home helps', computing and data processing, school transport, security, printing, fire brigades, police, civic amenity sites, pest control, dredging, and the operation of quarries and asphalt plants. Within the National Health Service, possibilities include not only domestic services, laundry and catering, but also portering, security, messenger work, ground maintenance, transport, ambulance services, medical records, computing, design, public relations, legal services, secretarial and clerical work, auditing, pharmacy and laboratory work, and pathology. In Denmark a company in the private sector provides almost half the fire protection and nearly all of the ambulance service. Examples of successful private fire and police services are to be found in the United States.

Extent of Competitive Tendering in Britain

So far only about one-tenth of the spending of local authorities is covered by CCT, although this is an improvement on the 1 per cent achieved in 1988. In Japan, by contrast, almost half of local authority services were contracted out as early as 1980. Extension of competitive tendering in local authorities to professional and technical services would be marginal but useful. Proposals to make it more difficult for obstructive councils to continue to deny the public the benefits of competition would certainly be beneficial. The addition by the European Economic Community of a further and overlapping set of rules is, however, not only unlikely to produce noticeable benefit, but will add to costs (and particularly so in the UK).

Extension of competitive tendering in the National Health Service would likewise be beneficial, and in central government departments a fresh impulse is needed. More radical thinking might be required, however, if the full advantages obtainable through competition are to be secured. The management of hospitals and of schools, for example, could usefully be made subject to competitive tendering on a limited, experimental basis.

The Size of Contracts

The size of contracts is a matter which needs more attention. Contracts need to be of sizes appropriate for those organisations able to do the work most efficiently. The tendency of many authorities is to package work in ways which suit their existing in-house works departments. Instead they should consult both internal and external contractors so as to discover the most economical arrangement. Even where contracts are packaged out of habit, or as a result of a vague belief in economies of scale, rather than as one way of favouring in-house provision, it can be contrary to the best interest of the client side and thereby of the public. In some of the larger authorities the client and in-house contractor sides are still too close to each other, and further separation is needed.

The Client Role and the Discovery of the Consumer

Councils spend far too little time on discussing the client role, on setting standards for services, improving monitoring and ensuring that they know what the results are. Instead, most of them spend far too much of their time on the contracting side of their organisations. Discovery of the consumer, and all that this implies, is as yet only in its early stages. If government and NHS consumers could take the money with them and buy elsewhere it would do wonders in changing the attitudes of authorities of all types. However, so long as their customers are captive these organisations will need constant reminding of who it is that supplies their incomes. Competitive tendering makes a double contribution, both by improving efficiency directly, and indirectly by improving organisation, management and attitudes.

Recommendations

(1) Competitive tendering for the management of a small number of hospitals should be introduced on a trial basis, subject to appropriate safeguards. Only by experiment will the usefulness or otherwise of such measures be discovered.

(2) The emphasis of council and health authority members should be less on the workings of the services provided by their organisations and more on the needs and problems to be met, the extent to which they are being met, and how they can be met more effectively.

(3) Authorities which have contracted out very few or none of the services subject to CCT (198 local authorities appear to be in this category in respect of the 1988 Act) either have unusually efficient in-house workforces, or they have protected them from competition in disregard of the legislation. This matter should be investigated by the Audit Commission and the results and conclusions published.

(4) Councils which do not use or propose to use in-house suppliers for a defined service are not at present affected in respect of that service by the CCT legislation. They should be required to use competitive tendering unless—and this is unlikely—they can show good reason why it should not be used. In other words, there should be a presumption in favour of competition whether or not there is an in-house workforce seeking to do the work.

(5) The very large size of some contracts is a matter for concern. Local and health authorities should be obliged to divide proposed contracts which are greater in size than a set level (dependent on the activity) into separate contracts for tendering purposes. This would permit either distribution of the work between different contractors or its amalgamation,

depending on which proves in practice to be more economical. Economies or diseconomies of scale should be discovered rather than assumed. Authorities should be encouraged to use market research to determine the contract packaging most conducive to efficient provision of services by existing and potential contractors, including where appropriate voluntary organisations.

(6) Consideration should be given to altering the *de minimis* figure, above which local authority work for a single activity is subject to compulsory competition. The Audit Commission should first assess the evidence for the figure of £100,000 being too high or too low.

(7) Direct service organisations should be free to buy the supplies they require competitively, rather than being tied to in-house provision. This is beginning to happen already, and its general adoption would be beneficial both to the DSOs and to the efficiency of other departments.

(8) Authorities should be encouraged to experiment, where appropriate, with inviting tenders for different levels of service rather than simply for a single specification. Market research should be used to discover those service levels which the public prefer when given knowledge of relative costs.

(9) Competitive tendering should gradually be extended to the fire services and to suitable aspects of police work so as to test and improve their efficiency.

(10) Directives from the European Economic Community require careful scrutiny lest they become an unnecessary burden as well as being a far greater burden in practice for local authorities in Britain than for those in other countries.

Bibliography/References

Note: Nearly all sources referred to in the text are listed in the bibliography, which also includes a few not otherwise mentioned.

AC86 (1986): Audit Commission, *Value for Money in the Fire Service: some strategic issues to be resolved*, London: HMSO.

AC87 (1987): Audit Commission, *Competitiveness and Contracting Out of Local Authorities' Services*, London: HMSO.

AC88a (1988): Audit Commission, *The Competitive Council*, London: HMSO.

AC88b (1988): Audit Commission, *Competitive Management of Parks and Green Spaces*, London: HMSO.

AC89a (1989): Audit Commission, *Preparing for Compulsory Competition*, London: HMSO.

AC89b (1989): Audit Commission, *Managing Cemeteries and Crematoria in a Competitive Environment*, London: HMSO.

AC90a (1990): Audit Commission, *Management Buy-outs: public interest or private gain?*, London: HMSO.

AC90b (1990): Audit Commission, *We Can't Go on Meeting Like This*, London: HMSO.

AC90c (1990): Audit Commission, *Managing Sickness Absence in London*, London: HMSO.

AC90d (1990): Audit Commission, *Building Maintenance DLOs in London*, London: HMSO.

AC91a (1991): Audit Commission, *The Impact of Competitive Tendering on Highways Maintenance*, London: HMSO.

AC91b (1991): Audit Commission, *Competitive Counsel? Using Lawyers in Local Government*, London: HMSO.

ALA: [Digings, Lee], *The Continental Challenge: European Compe-*

tition For Local Authority Services, London: Association of London Authorities, undated [1989?].

Alchian, Armen A. (1967): *Pricing and Society*, IEA Occasional Paper No. 17, London: Institute of Economic Affairs.

Allen, Joan W. *et al.* (1990): *The Private Sector in State Service Delivery: examples of innovative practices*, Lanham, Md.: University Press of America.

AMA (1991): *AMA response to the proposal for a Council Directive relating to services*, [London]: Association of Metropolitan Authorities.

Ascher, Kate (1987): *The Politics of Privatisation: Contracting Out Public Services*, Basingstoke, Hampshire: Macmillan Education.

Bach, Stephen (1989): *Too High a Price to Pay? A Study of Competitive Tendering for Domestic Services in the NHS*, Warwick Papers in Industrial Relations, No. 25, Coventry: Industrial Relations Research Unit, School of Industrial and Business Studies, University of Warwick.

Bach, Stephen (1990): 'Competitive tendering and contracting out: prospects for the future', in Cook, Haydn (ed.), *The NHS/Private Health Sector Interface*, Harlow, Essex: Longman.

Bennett, James T., & Manuel H. Johnson (1981): *Better Government at Half the Price: Private Production of Public Services*, Ottawa, Illinois: Caroline House Publishers, Inc.

Beresford, Paul (1987): *Good Council Guide: Wandsworth—1978-1987*, London: Centre for Policy Studies.

Blundell, John (1986): 'Privatization—by political process or consumer preference?', in *Economic Affairs*, October/November 1986, reprinted in Russell Lewis (ed.), *Recent Controversies in Political Economy*, London and New York: Routledge, 1992, pp. 226-33.

Bracewell-Milnes, Barry (1982): *Land and Heritage: The Public Interest in Personal Ownership*, Hobart Paper No. 93, London: Institute of Economic Affairs.

Bracewell-Milnes, Barry (1991): 'Earmarking in Britain: Theory and Practice', in Ranjit S. Teja and Barry Bracewell-Milnes, *The Case for Earmarked Taxes: Government Spending and Public Choice*, Research Monograph No. 46, London: Institute of Economic Affairs.

Burton, John (1983): *Picking Losers . . .?: The Political Economy of Industrial Policy*, Hobart Paper No. 99, London: Institute of Economic Affairs.

Burton, Michael (1991): 'Cross-boundary Tendering', *Municipal Journal*, 22 February, pp. 24-25.

Burton, Michael (1992a): 'The secret services', *Municipal Journal*, 17 January, pp. 10-11.

Burton, Michael (1992b): 'Stricken to the core,' *Municipal Journal*, 22 May, pp. 14-15.

Burton, Michael (1992c): 'Is the *de minimis* level too low?', *Municipal Journal*, 13 March, pp. 18-19.

Butler, Eamonn (ed.) (1988): *Privatization in Practice*, London: Adam Smith Institute.

Butler, Eamonn, Madsen Pirie and Peter Young (1985): *The Omega File*, London: Adam Smith Institute.

CAG (1991): National Audit Office, Report by the Comptroller and Auditor General, *Ministry of Defence: Initiatives in Defence Procurement*, London: HMSO.

CBI1 (1984): Confederation of British Industry, *Efficiency in the public services—2nd Report of the CBI Working Party on government current expenditure*, London: CBI.

CBI2 (1988): Confederation of British Industry, *The competitive advantage—Report of the CBI Public Expenditure Task Force*, London: CBI.

CBT: *Cross-Boundary Tendering* [Enforced Tendering Advice 3], [London]: Local Government Information Unit, undated.

CC (1986): *Contract Compliance: UK Experiences and Problems*, Manchester: Centre for Local Economic Strategies.

CCMA (1990): *The Facts on the NHS Privatisation Experience: A response to 'The NHS Privatisation Experience' by the Joint NHS Privatisation Research Unit*, London: Contract Cleaning and Maintenance Association.

CCRR (1992): *CCT Information Service: Client/Contractor Relationships Report 1992*, London: The Local Government Management Board.

CCS: *Contract Compliance Seminar Report*, Glasgow: Scottish Local Government Information Unit, undated [1987?].

CCT: *Compulsory Competitive Tendering: Advice for Labour Groups*, [London]: The Labour Party, undated [1990?].

CCT2 (1991): *Compulsory Competitive Tendering: Survey Report No. 2—Rounds 1-3*, Edinburgh: Convention of Scottish Local Authorities.

CCT&LMS: *Compulsory Competitive Tendering & Local Management of Schools*, [London]: Local Government Information Unit, undated [c1989].

CCTIS (1991): *CCT Information Service: Survey Report No. 4, December 1991*, London: The Local Government Management Board.

CCTLGA (1991): *Compulsory Competitive Tendering and the Local Government Act 1988* (2nd edition), London: Fox Williams (solicitors).

CFC (1990): *Contracts for Care: Briefing Paper No. 1*, London: Community Care Project, NCVO.

CH (1992): *The Contracts Handbook, Part Three 1992*, London: CD-C Research.

CH/B (1992): *The Contracts Handbook* [August 1992 edition], London: CD-C Publishing.

CL: *Consumer Liaison and Compulsory Tendering* [Enforced Tendering Advice 1], London: Local Government Information Unit, undated.

Clarke, Michael, & John Stewart (1988): *The Enabling Council: Developing and managing a new style of local government*, Luton: Local Government Training Board.

Clarke, Michael, & John Stewart (1989a): *The Councillor and the Enabling Council: Changing Roles*, Luton: Local Government Training Board.

Clarke, Michael, & John Stewart (1989b): *Challenging Old Assumptions: the enabling council takes shape*, Luton: Local Government Training Board.

COLG (1988): *Contracting-Out and the Local Government Act 1988*, London: Herbert Oppenheimer, Nathan & Vandyk.

COPS (1984): *Contracting Out in the Public Sector: Proceedings of a Conference*, London: Royal Institute of Public Administration.

Courcouf, Lesley (1991): 'Can CCT save money in the white-collar services?', *Municipal Journal*, 28 June, pp. 15 & 17.

CP: *Competition in Practice: A symposium on competitive tendering under the Local Government Act 1988*, London: The Public and Local Service Efficiency Campaign (PULSE), undated [1988?].

CQ (1991): *Competing for Quality. Competition in the Provision of Local Services: A Consultation Paper*, Department of the Environment/The Scottish Office/Welsh Office.

CQBB (1991): *Competing for Quality—Buying Better Public Services*, London: HMSO.

CQH (1992): *Competing for Quality in Housing. Competition in the Provision of Housing Management: A Consultation Paper*, Department of the Environment/Welsh Office.

Crowe, Virginia (ed.), *Equal Opportunities through Contract Compliance: the British and American experience*, National Symposium, 6-7 February 1986. A report by the ILEA Contract Compliance Equal Opportunities Unit. [London: ILEA, 1986?].

CTCC (1988): *Competitive Tendering and Contract Conditions: A Guide to the Local Government Act 1988*, London: Local Government Information Unit.

Cubbin, John, Simon Domberger & Shirley Meadowcroft (1987): 'Competitive Tendering and Refuse Collection: Identifying the Sources of Efficiency Gains', *Fiscal Studies*, Vol. 8, No. 3, August, pp. 49-58.

David, Irwin T. (1988): 'Privatization in America', *The Municipal Year Book 1988*, Washington, DC: International City/County Management Association [ICMA], pp. 43-55.

Davies, Howard, 'Obtaining Value for Money', in *Competition in Practice*, London: The Public and Local Service Efficiency Campaign, undated [1988?].

Davis, Dave (1985): *Public Hospitals, Private Management*, London: Adam Smith Institute/ASI (Research) Ltd.

DeHoog, Ruth Hoogland (1984): *Contracting Out for Human Services: economic, political, and organizational perspectives*, Albany: State University of New York Press.

Digings, Lee (1991): *Competitive Tendering and the European Communities: Public Procurement, CCT and Local Services*, London: Association of Metropolitan Authorities.

Domberger, S., S. A. Meadowcroft & D. J. Thompson (1986): 'Competitive Tendering and Efficiency: The Case of Refuse Collection', *Fiscal Studies*, Vol. 7, No. 4, November, pp. 69-87.

Domberger, Simon, Shirley Meadowcroft & David Thompson (1987): 'The Impact of Competitive Tendering on the Costs of Hospital Domestic Services', *Fiscal Studies*, Vol. 8, No. 4, November, pp. 39-54.

Domberger, Simon, Shirley Meadowcroft & David Thompson (1988): 'Competition and Efficiency in Refuse Collection: A Reply', *Fiscal Studies*, Vol. 9, No. 1, February, pp. 86-90.

DP (1988): *Don't Panic! A guide for councillors and officers on how to deal with compulsory tendering under the Local Government (No 2) Bill 1987*, AMA/LGIU/LSPU/ADLO.

EC92: 'Council Directive 92/50/EEC of 18 June 1992 relating to the coordination of procedures for the award of public service contracts', *Official Journal of the European Communities no. L 209, 24.7.92*, pp. 1-24.

ECD (1991): *The EC Directives: and their effect on work subject to compulsory competition in local government in the UK*, London: The Chartered Institute of Public Finance and Accountancy (An Occasional Paper by the Competition Joint Committee).

EO: *Equal Opportunities and CCT: A contradiction in terms?* (Enforced Tendering Advice 4), London: Local Government Information Unit, undated.

ETPP (1967): *Essays in the Theory and Practice of Pricing*, Readings in Political Economy No. 3, London: Institute of Economic Affairs.

Evans, Timothy (ed.) (1991): *An Arresting Idea: The Management of Police Services in Modern Britain*, London: Adam Smith Institute/ASI (Research) Limited.

Finley, Lawrence K. (ed.) (1989): *Public Sector Privatization: alternative approaches to service delivery*, Westport, Conn.: Quorum Books.

Fitzgerald, Randall (1988): *When Government Goes Private: successful alternatives to public services*, New York, NY: Universe Books (a Pacific Research Institute for Public Policy Book).

Fixler Jr., Philip E. (1986): *Another service shedding option for local governments—nonprofit and voluntary organizations*, Santa Monica, California: Reason Foundation.

Flynn, Norman, & Kieron Walsh (1988): *Competitive Tendering*, Birmingham: Institute of Local Government Studies, University of Birmingham.

Forsyth, Michael (1981): *Re-servicing Britain*, London: Adam Smith Institute, 2nd edition.

Gage, Theodore (1982): 'Cops, Inc.', *Reason*, November, pp. 23-28.

Ganley, Joe & John Grahl (1988): 'Competition and Efficiency in Refuse Collection: A Critical Comment', *Fiscal Studies*, Vol. 9, No. 1, February, pp. 80-85.

GCD: *The Guide to Competition in Defence Services*, The Contracting Out Unit, Ministry of Defence, undated.

GLC (1983): *The Contract Clean-up: An outline of trends and conditions in the contract cleaning industry*, [London]: GLC, Economic Policy Group—Strategy document No. 9.

Gray, Hamish (1968): *The Cost of Council Housing*, Research Monograph No. 18, London: Institute of Economic Affairs.

Green, David (1990): *It Can All Be Done Better*, Okehampton, Devon: District Council Technical Association.

Griffith, Ben, Steve Iliffe & Geof Rayner (1987): *Banking on Sickness: Commercial Medicine in Britain and the USA*, London: Lawrence and Wishart.

Gutch, Richard (1989): 'Should voluntary services tender?', *Municipal Journal*, 28 July, pp. 43 & 45.

Hall, John, *A Statement on the difficulties experienced by contractors working with Government Departments*, London: Aims of Industry, undated.

Harris, Ralph, and Arthur Seldon (1959/1962): *Advertising in a Free Society*, and *Advertising and the Public*, London: André Deutsch for the Institute of Economic Affairs.

Hartley, Keith (1980): 'The Economics of Bureaucracy and Local Government', in *Town Hall Power or Whitehall Pawn?*, IEA Readings No. 25, London: Institute of Economic Affairs.

Hartley, Keith (1984): 'Why contract out?', in *Contracting Out in the Public Sector*, Proceedings of a Conference, London: Royal Institute of Public Administration.

Hartley, Keith, & Meg Huby (1985): 'Contracting-Out in Health and

Local Authorities: prospects, progress and pitfalls', *Public Money*, September, pp. 23-26.

Hartley, Keith (1991): 'Public Purchasing', *Public Money & Management*, Spring, pp. 45-49.

Hatry, Harry P. (1983): *A Review of Private Approaches for Delivery of Public Services*, Washington, DC: The Urban Institute Press.

Healy, Maurice, & Jenny Potter (1987): 'Making Performance Measurement Work for Consumers', in *Performance Measurement and the Consumer*, London: National Consumer Council.

Hirsch, Werner Z. (1991): *Privatizing government services: an economic analysis of contracting out by local governments*, Los Angeles: Institute of Industrial Relations, University of California.

HMT (1986): HM Treasury, *Using Private Enterprise in Government: Report of a multi-departmental review of competitive tendering and contracting for services in Government Departments*, London: HMSO.

HMT (1991): HM Treasury, *Government Purchasing: progress report to the Prime Minister 1990*, London: HMSO.

Holliday, Ian (1991): 'The New Suburban Right in British Local Government—Conservative Views of the Local', *Local Government Studies*, November/December, pp. 45-62.

Howes, Stephen and Craig Inglis (1991): 'Are direct service organisations heading down the precipice?', *Municipal Journal*, 1 March, pp. 24-25.

HPSS (1991): *Health and Personal Social Services Statistics for England*, 1991 edition, London: HMSO.

IDS (1988): *Competitive Tendering in the Public Sector*, [London]: Institute of Personnel Management & Incomes Data Services Public Sector Unit, Revised edition.

Itani, Minoru (1989): 'The privatisation of local authority services in Japan', *Planning and Administration*, Vol. 16, No. 2, Autumn, pp. 51-58.

Ivens, Michael (1992): *The Disease of Direct Labour: Buying Better for the Public*, London: Centre for Policy Studies.

Jackson, P. M. (1987): 'Value for Money—Whose value is it anyway?', in *Performance Measurement and the Consumer*, London: National Consumer Council.

Keenan, Paul (1991): 'The hands of the professionals', *Local Government Chronicle*, 5 July, pp. 18-20.

Kemp, Roger L. (ed.) (1991): *Privatization: the provision of public services by the private sector*, Jefferson, North Carolina: McFarland & Company.

Kerley, Richard & Douglas Wynn (1990): *Competitive Tendering: The Transition to Contracted Service Provision in Scottish Local Authorities*, Glasgow: Scottish Local Authorities Management Centre.

Kerley, Richard, & Douglas Wynn (1991): 'Competitive Tendering— The Transition to Contracting in Scottish Local Authorities', *Local Government Studies*, September/October, pp. 33-51. (This is a revised and shortened version of the same authors' publication of 1990.)

Knox, Frank, and Jossleyn Hennessy (1966): *Restrictive Practices in the Building Industry*, Research Monograph No. 1, London: Institute of Economic Affairs.

Kristensen, Ole P. (1983): 'Public Versus Private Provision of Governmental Services: The Case of Danish Fire Protection Services', *Urban Studies*, Vol. 20, pp. 1-9.

Kunz, Christian, Rowan Jones and Ken Spencer (1989): *Bidding for Change? Voluntary Organisations and Competitive Tendering for Local Authority Services following the Local Government Act, 1988*, Birmingham: Birmingham Settlement Research Unit.

Lait, June (1980): 'Central Government's Ineptitude in Monitoring Local Welfare', in *Town Hall Power or Whitehall Pawn?*, IEA Readings No. 25, London: Institute of Economic Affairs.

LGA (1988): *Local Government Act 1988*, London: HMSO.

LGA92 (1992): *Local Government Act 1992*, London: HMSO.

LGAC (1988): *Local Government Act 1988: Part I and Schedule I. Competition in the Provisions of Local Authority Services*, circular 19/88 from the Department of the Environment, 8 August, London: HMSO.

LGAFO (1991): *Local Government Act 1988 Financial Objectives (England) (Amendment) Specifications 1991*, London: Department of the Environment.

LGANCM (1988): *Local Government Act 1988—Public Supply and*

Works Contracts: Non-Commercial Matters, circular 8/88 (Department of the Environment); circular 12/88 (Welsh Office), 6 April, London: HMSO.

LGC89 (1989): *Local Government Chronicle*, 7 July, pp. 8-17.

LGC90 (1990): *Local Government Chronicle*, 6 July, pp. 12-15.

LGIU (1990): *LGIU Briefing*, July/August, London: Local Government Information Unit.

LGPLA (1980): *Local Government, Planning and Land Act 1980*, London: HMSO.

McDavid, James C. (1985): 'The Canadian Experience with Privatizing Residential Solid Waste Collection Services', *Public Administration Review*, September/October, pp. 602-608.

McDavid, James (1988): 'Privatizing Local Government Services in Canada', in *Privatization: Tactics and Techniques* (Proceedings of a symposium held 22-24 July 1987, in Vancouver, BC), Vancouver, BC: Fraser Institute.

McGuirk, Tom (1992): *The Competitive Edge: 'A study of early trends in CCT under the 1988 Local Government Act'*, Croydon: Institute of Public Finance.

Marlin, John Tepper (1982): *Privatisation of Local Government Activities: Lessons from Japan*, London: Aims of Industry.

Marsland, David (1980): 'Three Fallacies: Ideological Error in Local Government Thinking?', in *Town Hall Power or Whitehall Pawn?*, IEA Readings No. 25, London: Institute of Economic Affairs.

Martin, Lawrence L. (1992): 'A Proposed Methodology for Comparing the Costs of Government versus Contract Service Delivery', *The Municipal Year Book 1992*, Washington, DC: International City/County Management Association [ICMA], pp. 12-15.

Mather, Graham (1991): *Government by Contract*, IEA Inquiry No. 25, March, London: Institute of Economic Affairs; *Public Money and Management*, Autumn 1990, pp. 5-6, 9-16.

Maude, Francis (1992): *Financial Secretary's speech to the Adam Smith Institute conference on contracting out for central government services*, London: HM Treasury (press notice 20/92).

Maynard, Alan K., and David N. King (1972): *Rates or Prices?*, Hobart Paper No. 54, London: Institute of Economic Affairs.

MBOLG (1991): *Management Buy-outs in Local Government: Salvation or Shambles?*, London: Local Government Information Unit.

MCF (1986): *More Contractors' Failures*, London: Trades Union Congress.

Meredith, Simon (1992): 'Bring in the cognoscenti,' *Personal Computer Magazine*, August, pp. 220-26.

Milne, Robin G. (1987): 'Competitive Tendering in the NHS: an economic analysis of the early implementation of HC(83)18', *Public Administration*, Vol. 65, No. 2, Summer, pp. 145-60.

MTBI (1992): *Market Testing and Buying In*, London: HM Treasury, (Public Competition and Purchasing Unit—Guidance No. 34).

NAO (1987): National Audit Office, Report by the Comptroller and Auditor General, *Competitive Tendering for Support Services in the National Health Service*, London: HMSO.

NALGO (1987): *Fighting Privatisation: The campaign to defend and improve the NHS*, NALGO.

NCVO (1991): *Contracting In or Out?*, Summer, London: National Council for Voluntary Organisations.

Newbigging, Rosie, & John Lister (1988): *The record of private companies in NHS support services*, London: London Health Emergency, and Association of London Authorities.

PA: *The Management of Change in Local Authorities: A Joint Survey on Change and Management Practices in Local Government*, London: PA Consulting Group, undated [1989/90].

PAC (1990): *Privatisation and cuts: the government record*, London: Labour Research Department.

Paddon, Michael (1991): 'Management Buy-outs and Compulsory Competition in Local Government', *Local Government Studies*, May/June, pp. 27-52.

PAE: *Policy Analysis and Evaluation*. Proceedings of Seminar A held at the PTRC Summer Annual Meeting, University of Sussex, England, from 10-13 July 1984 (Volume P244).

Paine, Leslie (1984): 'Contracting Out in the Bethlem Royal and Maudsley Hospitals', in *Contracting Out in the Public Sector*, Proceedings of a Conference, London: Royal Institute of Public Administration.

Painter, Joe (1990): *Seconds Out, Round Two: The first round of compulsory competitive tendering*, Manchester: Centre for Local Economic Strategies.

Painter, Joe (1991): 'Compulsory Competitive Tendering in Local Government: The First Round', *Public Administration*, Vol. 69, Summer, pp. 191-210.

Papps, Ivy (1975): *Government and Enterprise*, Hobart Paper No. 61, London: Institute of Economic Affairs.

Parker, David, & Keith Hartley (1990a): 'Competitive Tendering: Issues and Evidence', *Public Money and Management*, Autumn, pp. 9-16.

Parker, David (1990b): 'The 1988 Local Government Act and Compulsory Competitive Tendering', *Urban Studies*, Vol. 27, No. 5, October, pp. 653-68.

PCLG (1991): *Provision for Competition in Local Government*, Department of the Environment.

PCPC (1985): *The Public Cost of Private Contractors*, London: Services to Community Action and Trade Unions (SCAT).

PCR: *Privatisation Conference Report*, [Glasgow: Scottish Local Government Information Unit], undated [1986?].

PE (1990): *The Privatisation Experience: Competitive tendering for NHS services*, London: The Joint NHS Privatisation Research Unit.

Phillips, Lesley (1990): 'Local authority management buyouts', *Management Accounting*, March, p. 9.

Pirie, Madsen (1988): *Privatization: Theory, Practice and Choice*, London: Adam Smith Institute.

Pirie, Madsen (1988): *Privatization*, Aldershot, Hants.: Wildwood House.

Pirie, Madsen, and Eamonn Butler (1989): *Extending Care*, London: Adam Smith Institute.

PJPP (1983): *Public Jobs for Private Profit: Fighting contractors in Wandsworth*, London: Wandsworth Trade Union Publications.

Pollard, Mark (1990): 'Compulsory, competitive tendering: year one', *Municipal Journal*, 2 November, pp. 22-23.

Poole, Jr., Robert W. (1980): *Cutting Back City Hall*, New York, NY: Universe Books.

Poole, Jr., Robert W. (1983): 'Objections to Privatization', reprinted from *Policy Review* (The Heritage Foundation, Washington, DC), Spring.

POP (1982): *Public or Private: The case against privatisation*, London: Labour Research Department/LRD Publications Ltd.

PP (1988): *Privatising Portering*, London: Joint NHS Privatisation Research Unit.

PPP (1987): *Privatisation: Paying the Price*, London: Labour Research Department/LRD Publications Ltd.

PR (1991): Haarmeyer, David (ed.), *Privatization 1991*, Santa Monica, California: Reason Foundation.

PSA (1991): 'Contract analysis', *Public Service Action*, February, Sheffield: SCAT Publications.

PSR: *Public Service Review*, London: Public and Local Service Efficiency Campaign (PULSE), various issues [undated].

PTSE (1989): *Privatisation: The Scottish Experience*, [Edinburgh?]: Edinburgh Health Service Campaign.

PTT (1988): *Privatization: Tactics and Techniques*. Proceedings of a symposium held 22-24 July 1987, in Vancouver, BC, Vancouver, BC: The Fraser Institute.

PSCR (1991): *The Public Supply Contracts Regulations 1991*, Statutory Instrument 1991 No. 2679, London: HMSO.

PWCR (1991): *The Public Works Contracts Regulations 1991*, Statutory Instrument 1991 No. 2680, London: HMSO.

QS: *Quality Street: Labour's quality programme for local government*, London: The Labour Party, undated [1989?]

RC: *Refuse Collection and Street Cleaning Services: a report on the competition and experience of privatisation: Company Profiles*, Sheffield: Sheffield City Council, undated [1990].

Rehfuss, John A. (1989): *Contracting Out in Government: A Guide to Working with Outside Contractors to Supply Public Services*, San Francisco: Jossey-Bass.

Ridley, Nicholas (1988): *The Local Right: enabling not providing*, London: Centre for Policy Studies.

Rix, Cecil (1984): 'Contracting out: contract management', in *Contracting Out in the Public Sector*, London: Royal Institute of Public Administration.

Robertson, Douglas (1992): 'The Contracting Out of Legal Services within the Public Sector', *Public Money & Management*, April-June, pp. 53-56.

Savas, E. S. (1987): *Privatization: The Key to Better Government*, Chatham, New Jersey: Chatham House Publishers.

SDE (1992): *Statement on the Defence Estimates 1992*, London: HMSO. Also the same publication for earlier years.

Seader, David (1986): 'Privatization and America's Cities', *Public Management*, December, pp. 6-9.

Seldon, Arthur (1977): *Charge*, London: Temple Smith.

SGLGA (1988): *A Scottish Guide to the Local Government Act 1988*, Glasgow: Scottish Local Government Information Unit.

Shann, Ed (1990): 'Tender debate deserves a fair hearing', *Business Review Weekly* (Australia), 26 October, p. 42.

Sheaff, Mike (1988): 'NHS ancillary services and competitive tendering', *Industrial Relations Journal*, Vol. 19, No. 2, Summer, pp. 93-105.

Shenfield, Arthur *et al.* (1983): *Public Services and the Private Alternative*, London: Adam Smith Institute.

Simmonds, Michael (1989): *The Burning Question*, London: Adam Smith Institute/ASI (Research) Limited.

SITH: *Safe in their hands: the record of private contractors in public services*, London: Cleaning and Support Services Association, undated [1991?].

SLG (1990): 'Tendering costs jobs', *Scottish Local Government*, October, Glasgow: Scottish Local Government Information Unit.

Spencer, Ken (1984): 'The privatisation and contracting out of local government services', in *Policy Analysis and Evaluation*. Proceedings of Seminar A held at the PTRC Summer Annual Meeting, University of Sussex, England, from 10-13 July (Volume P244).

TT (1990): *The Tender Traps*, London: Adam Smith Institute.

TTCL (1988): *Taken to the Cleaners: The Lincolnshire Experience*, Nottingham: NUPE (East Midlands Division) and NALGO (East Midlands Division).

Veljanovski, Cento (ed.) (1989): *Privatisation and Competition: A Market Prospectus*, Hobart Paperback No. 28, London: Institute of Economic Affairs.

Walker, Jill, & Roger Moore (1983): *Privatisation of Local Government Services*, Workers' Educational Association.

Walsh, Annmarie (1988): 'Designing and Managing the Procurement Process', *IPA Report*, Spring, pp. 3-7, New York, NY: Institute of Public Administration.

Walsh, Kieron (1991): *Competitive Tendering for Local Authority Services: Initial Experiences*, London: HMSO.

Whitworth, Brian (1984): 'The Contracting Out Choice and Review of In-House Services: The Role of External Consultancy', in *Contracting Out in the Public Sector*, Proceedings of a Conference, London: Royal Institute of Public Administration.

Wigginton, Michael (1991): 'Compulsory competitive tendering: what difference will it make to design?', *RSA Journal*, December, pp. 7-9.

Willis, Eric (1990): 'The alternative approach to solving the problem of fraud', *Management Accounting*, March, pp. 26-27.

Willson, Michael (1991): 'Contracting Corruption', *Local Government Studies*, May/June, pp. 1-6.

Winetrobe, Barry, & Celia Nield (1987): *Local Government Bill [Bill 2, 1987-88]: Competitive Tendering and Contract Compliance* (Reference Sheet no. 87/3), [London]: House of Commons Library Research Division.

WWC (1982): *Working with Contractors*, London: Adam Smith Institute.

Zetter, John (1984): 'The privatisation of urban services', in *Policy Analysis and Evaluation*. Proceedings of Seminar A held at the PTRC Summer Annual Meeting, University of Sussex, England, from 10-13 July (Volume P244).

Some organisations referred to in the text

ASI—Adam Smith Institute

ADC—Association of District Councils

AHST—Association of Health Service Treasurers

AMA—Association of Metropolitan Authorities

Audit Commission for Local Authorities and the National Health Service in England and Wales—Audit Commission (formerly the Audit Commission for Local Authorities in England and Wales)

Central Unit on Purchasing (a department in HM Treasury)

CLES—Centre for Local Economic Strategies

CPS—Centre for Policy Studies

Centre for Public Services (formerly Services to Community Action and Trade Unions)

CIPFA—Chartered Institute of Public Finance and Accountancy

CSSA—Cleaning and Support Services Association (formerly the Contract Cleaning and Maintenance Association)

CSA—Common Services Agency (Scotland)

CSA—Common Services Authority (Wales)

Commission for Local Authority Accounts in Scotland

CBI—Confederation of British Industry

CCMA—Contract Cleaning and Maintenance Association (former name of the Cleaning and Support Services Association)

COSLA—Convention of Scottish Local Authorities

DOE—Department of the Environment

DHSS—Department of Health and Social Security (since divided into the Department of Health and the Department of Social Security)

DICTA—District Council Technical Association

Efficiency Unit (within the Cabinet Office)

INLOGOV—Institute of Local Government Studies (at the University of Birmingham)

IPF—Institute of Public Finance Ltd (a company owned by CIPFA)

Joint NHS Privatisation Research Unit

LRD—Labour Research Department

LGIU—Local Government Information Unit

LGMB—Local Government Management Board

LGTB—Local Government Training Board (now merged with the Local Government Management Board)

London Health Emergency

MoD—Ministry of Defence

NAO—National Audit Office

NCVO—National Council for Voluntary Organisations

NHS—National Health Service

NALGO—National and Local Government Officers' Association

Public Competition and Purchasing Unit (the name adopted by the Central Unit on Purchasing from November 1991 to April 1992)

PULSE—Public and Local Service Efficiency Campaign

Public Services Privatisation Research Unit

SHHD—Scottish Home and Health Department

Scottish Local Authorities Management Centre (at the Strathclyde Graduate Business School, University of Strathclyde)

SCAT—Services to Community Action and Trade Unions (name changed in 1991 to Centre for Public Services)

TUC—Trades Union Congress

Welsh Office

Abbreviations in use in addition to the above:

CCT—compulsory competitive tendering

DHA—district health authority

DLO—direct labour organisation

DSO—direct service organisation

HB—health board